Seeing the Story of the Bible

SEEING THE STORY
OF THE BIBLE

by
MYER PEARLMAN

*with charts and
diagrams*

GOSPEL PUBLISHING HOUSE
Springfield, Missouri
02-0581

21st Printing 2002

International Standard Book Number 0-88243-581-7

Printed in the United States of America

CONTENTS

INTRODUCTION

A visitor to New York was endeavoring to become acquainted with that great city. He traveled down the long avenues, visited the outstanding public buildings and the main parks, and did his best to "take in" the city. He enjoyed his trips; but yet he was dissatisfied. The city was so large and his time was so limited. He would have to leave without seeing *all* of the city. A friend one day suggested an airplane ride. They ascended and saw New York spread out beneath their gaze. The friend acted the part of the guide. He showed the old and new sections of the city. He explained the plan on which it was built, and indicated its main divisions. Then before descending he pointed out the principal buildings, avenues, parks. harbor and other outstanding places of interest. Our vistor was content; he had seen New York city *as a whole*, and had received an impression of its size, construction, and beauty that he could impart to his friends.

Many Christians have been sight-seeing, so to speak, through the Bible. They have read a book, a chapter. a verse at a time—here a little, there a little. But they have not seen it as one great book with one plan. Now let us follow a different method. We are going to see the Bible as from a great height, and obtain a panoramic view of the sixty-six books and their contents. We shall note the two great divisions, the Old and New Testaments, and their relationship. We shall consider the progress of the divine plan in the Scriptures, studying the main sections instead of the individual books, and emphasizing the high points instead of the details.

When Satan, with evil motive, desired to impress Jesus with the glory of earthly kingdoms, he took Him to a high mountain and in a moment of time gave Him a sweeping, panoramic view of the whole. In order that John the Revelator might obtain a vision of the New Jerusalem in the fulness of its radiant beauty and faultless symmetry, and that he might view it in relation to all the nations of the earth, he was carried in spirit to a great and high mountain. In like manner, may this "aeroplane" study of the Scriptures increase our appreciation of their beauty and add to our understanding of the Divine purpose that pervades them.

Seeing the Story

A superficial reading of the Bible shows it to be a collection of sixty-six books written during a period of about sixteen hundred years by about forty different authors, among whom were kings, prophets, priests, a shepherd, and fishermen. It appears to be a library rather than one book. A first reading may not disclose a predominant theme, for the unity of the Scriptures does not appear on the surface. Rather, there will present itself to the reader a mingling of history, poetry, proverb, genealogy, law, prophecy, doctrine, and biography. The impression is that of a garment of many pieces and colors, rather than of one made from a single piece and woven without seam.

But as we read the Bible repeatedly and study it carefully, and as we penetrate below the surface and observe the unifying forces there, we discover that through the many stories and variegated subject matter of the Scriptures there runs one outstanding story and one predominant theme—The Redemption of Mankind Through a Divinely Appointed Saviour; and that all the human authors were under the direction of one Author—the Holy Spirit. (See Figure 1 on page 11.) Here we have a feature that makes the Bible so different from the sacred books of other religions: it has one predominant theme and a consistent plan running through it from the first to the last book. It is so different, for example, from the Mohammedan Koran, which consists of a collection of one hundred and fourteen unrelated chapters arranged according to their length. Our growing acquaintance with the Bible impresses us that its unity is not artificial, simply produced by editing and piecing together different fragments, but is ingrained in the very substance of the history as part of its texture. It is like a watermark which cannot be destroyed without ruining the paper.

The story which produces this unity is a dramatic story. "You make religion so dramatic," said a Jewish Rabbi to a missionary in answer to a question concerning the success and influence of Christianity. His witness is true. The redemption of the race does not depend upon a cold, formal system of ethics or philosophy, the product of careful, calculating reasonings of scholars. It has for its foundation a gripping story that has never failed, and never will fail, to stir the highest emotions of the human heart. The plan is well known. In the beginning man is separated from his Creator by that arch-villain of the universe, Satan, who consistently attempts to prevent a reconciliation. He is de-

REDEMPTION OF MAN

Genesis   Revelation

LA
HIS
TORY
POE
TRY
PRO
PHECY
BIO
GRAPHY
GENE
ALOGY
DOC
TRINE
PRO
VERBS
HYM
NS

Figure 1. Unity in Diversity

feated by that great Friend of humanity, the Lord Jesus, who makes the supreme sacrifice to deliver the race. The concluding chapters of the Bible give us a picture of the destruction of the great enemy, and of the redeemed eternally united to God in a new Eden that shall never pass away.

The plan of redemption is contained in a true story which satisfies not only the heart, but also the mind. "Tell us a *story* about God," has been the cry of simple souls throughout all ages. "Give us the *truth* about God" has been the demand of the learned. The Bible meets both of these demands by presenting *a true story*—the story of redemption through Christ.

It is a story the full purpose and details of which were not always understood by the authors.[1]   The great Author assigned different portions of the story to various writers, without letting them apprehend the plan in its completeness. Also, it is a drama in which many of the actors did not understand the

---

(1) Dan. 12:8, 9.—8 And I heard, but I understood not: then said I, O my Lord, what shall be the end of these things? 9 And he said, Go thy way, Daniel: for the words are closed up and sealed till the time of the end.

1 Peter 1:10, 11.—10 Of which salvation the prophets have enquired and searched diligently, who prophesied of the grace that should come unto you: 11 Searching what, or what manner of time the Spirit of Christ which was in them did signify, when it testified beforehand the sufferings of Christ, and the glory that should follow.

Matt. 13:17.—For verily I say unto you, That many prophets and righteous men have desired to see those things which ye see, and have not seen them; and to hear those things which ye hear, and have not heard them.

part they were playing, but their actions, whether good or evil, were woven into the plan.[2] Pharaoh, Nebuchadnezzar, Judas, Pilate, and others were ignorant of the fact that they were playing a role in the greatest of all dramas, as it was superintended by the great Author behind the scenes.

Redemption is a plan not defeated by outward failure. "It is in the depths of adversity and seeming defeat that it asserts itself most clearly, enlarges, purifies and spiritualizes itself, and is never, as in the prophets, more confident of victory than when, to the eye of sense, the cause of the kingdom of God seems hopelessly lost."—Orr.

" . . . ALL THE SCRIPTURES . . . CONCERNING HIM . . . "—LUKE 24:27.

The story of redemption finds its center in Christ, whose cross becomes its symbol. It is the living Christ to whom all the Scriptures point, and He it is who gives unity to the many stories and different varieties of subject matter. (See Figure 2 on page 15.) A heap of scrap iron is without vital unity in the mass, for the pieces are of different shapes, sizes, and colors. An electro-magnet is lowered, the power is turned on and immediately

---

(2) Acts 2:23.—23 Him, being delivered by the determinate counsel and foreknowledge of God, ye have taken, and by wicked hands have crucified and slain.

Acts 3:17, 18.—17 And now, brethren, I wot that through ignorance ye did it, as did also your rulers. 18 But those things, which God before had shewed by the mouth of all his prophets, that Christ should suffer, he hath so fulfilled.

every piece is animated, so to speak, with one spirit and purpose; all leap to the poles of the magnet and there become one—united in their movement toward a common center. In like manner, when the Redeemer was manifested—that great Spiritual Magnet—all scriptures, whether dealing with law, history, poetry or any other subject, were immediately drawn to Him as their center of unity.[3]   So then, borrowing the language of John 12:32, we may imagine the Lord saying, "And I, if I be lifted up from the earth, will draw all the *Scriptures* unto me."

TWO TESTAMENTS—ONE STORY

A first reading of the Bible might convey the impression that there was little connection between the two divisions, the Old and New Testaments; that they differ in many respects, for example, in some instances as to standards of conduct.   But a deeper study will disclose a unifying force that makes them really one book.   Europe and America are separated by the Atlantic ocean; but under the ocean the continents are joined together— forming one great continent.   So it is with the Scriptures.   As we look beneath the superficial differences caused by the various dispensational dealings with man, the pro-

---

(3) Luke 24:27.—27 And beginning at Moses and all the prophets, he expounded unto them in all the scriptures the things concerning himself.

Acts 10:43.—43 To him give all the prophets witness, that through his name whosoever believeth in him shall receive remission of sins.

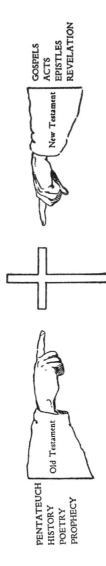

Figure 2. Christ the Center of all Scriptures

Figure 3. The New Testament is the Flower of the Old

gressiveness of revelation, the different customs, and so on, we discover a bond of unity that makes them really one volume. That unifying factor is God's redemptive purpose through a Redeemer.

The relationship between the Testaments is expressed by the statement that the Old Testament is fulfilled by the New. The Old Testament is completed by the New Testament just as the plant is completed by the flower. The New Testament develops from the Old as the blossom develops from the rest of the plant. (See Fig. 3 on page 16.) Until the blossom comes, the plant looks toward the *future*, it gives the *promise* of the flower. So in the Old Testament, Redemption is a great promise to be realized at a future time. And just as everything that goes to make a complete flower is contained in the seed which produces stem and bud, so before the gospel was ever preached, it existed in germ in the Old Testament. It was here that Paul found it, for the Old Testament was the Bible from which he preached the gospel. Upon it he based the fundamental doctrines of grace.[4] He insisted that the gospel he proclaimed was not a novelty, but was a message based upon the Law and the Prophets.[5]

---

(4) Rom. 3:21, 22.—21 But now the righteousness of God without the law is manifested, being witnessed by the law and the prophets; 22 Even the righteousness of God which is by faith of Jesus Christ unto all and upon all them that believe: for there is no difference.
(5) Acts 26:22, 23.—22 Having therefore obtained help of

Likewise the Epistle to the Hebrews is one grand demonstration that the outlines and characteristics of the gospel are contained in the institutions of the Old Testament.

The bud passes away, yet it is not destroyed; rather it finds its completion in the flower. The bud simply fulfills its purpose when it opens into the full flower. The Old Testament finds its completion in the New Testament and its Christ, and all that is imperfect, temporary, and provisional falls away of its own accord, while all that is permanent and essential remains. We can say that the Old Testament has passed away, particularly that Covenant which gives the book its name.[6]

God, I continue unto this day, witnessing both to small and great, saying none other things than those which the prophets and Moses did say should come: 23 That Christ should suffer, and that he should be the first that should rise from the dead, and should shew light unto the people, and to the Gentiles.

(6) Heb. 8:7-13.—7 For if that first covenant had been faultless, then should no place have been sought for the second. 8 For finding fault with them, he saith, Behold, the days come, saith the Lord, when I will make a new covenant with the house of Israel and with the house of Judah: 9 Not according to the covenant that I made with their fathers in the day when I took them by the hand to lead them out of the land of Egypt; because they continued not in my covenant, and I regarded them not, saith the Lord. 10 For this is the covenant that I will make with the house of Israel after those days, saith the Lord; I will put my laws into their mind, and write them in their hearts: and I will be to them a God, and they shall be to me a people: 11 And they shall not teach every man his neighbour, and every man his brother, saying, Know the Lord: for all shall know me, from the least to the greatest. 12 For I will be merciful to their unrighteousness, and their sins and their iniquities will I remember no more. 13 In that he saith, A new covenant, he hath made the first old. Now that which decayeth and waxeth old is ready to vanish away.

But it would not be correct to say that it has been destroyed by Christ and is therefore to be ignored or neglected or lightly esteemed.[7]

The plant does not attain its greatest usefulness until the bud has opened and all can admire its beauty and enjoy its fragrance. So in the Old Testament the truths of Redemption were sealed up, so to speak, in one nation, Israel, which nation was for the time the center of God's plan and the custodian of those truths.[8]   But when the Old Testament was fulfilled by Christ, the fragrance and beauty of all redemptive truth predicted and foreshadowed in the Old Testament were given to the whole world, to be enjoyed by "whosoever will."   Hence the last commission of the great Fulfiller was, "Go ye *into all the world* and preach the gospel *to every creature."*

Again, we may compare the two Testaments in this way:

---

(7) Matt. 5:17, 18.—17 Think not that I am come to destroy the law, or the prophets: I am not come to destroy, but to fulfill. 18 For verily I say unto you, Till heaven and earth pass, one jot or one tittle shall in no wise pass from the law, till all be fulfilled.

(8) Matt. 10:6.—6 But go rather to the lost sheep of the house of Israel.

Matt. 15:24.—24 But he answered and said, I am not sent but unto the lost sheep of the house of Israel.

Rom. 9:4, 5.—4 Who are Israelites; to whom pertaineth the adoption, and the glory and the covenants, and the giving of the law, and the service of God, and the promises; 5 Whose are the fathers, and of whom as concerning the flesh Christ came, who is over all, God blessed for ever. Amen.

OLD TESTAMENT	NEW TESTAMENT
Redemption promised and predicted.	Redemption accomplished.
Many animal sacrifices that could not take away sin forever.	The one, eternal sacrifice that makes perfect atonement.
Many human, imperfect priests.	The one perfect Divine Priest.
A new covenant promised.	The New Covenant instituted.
God's coming kingdom predicted.	God's kingdom at hand.
God's king, the Messiah, promised in type and prediction.	The birth, ministry, death, and resurrection of Jesus the Messiah and King.

HOW CHRIST FULFILLS THE SCRIPTURE

As we trace the story through the Old Testament and into the New, we see the truths of Redemption reaching mankind through *one nation,* Israel. These truths are fulfilled and stripped of their Old Testament wrappings (ceremonies, types, etc.) by *one person,* Christ. Finally, Christ sends these blessings to *all nations* by the Church. (See Fig. 4, page 21.) Further details of this progression show that:

In Old Testament times it was the privilege of the few to prophesy and to proclaim the supreme prophetic message, the coming of Messiah. Our Lord appeared as the perfect prophet bringing to mankind God's final and perfect message.[9] The privilege of prophesy-

(9) Deut. 18:18, 19.—18 I will raise them up a Prophet from among their brethren, like unto thee and will put my words in his mouth; and he shall speak unto them all that I shall command him. 19 And it shall come to pass,

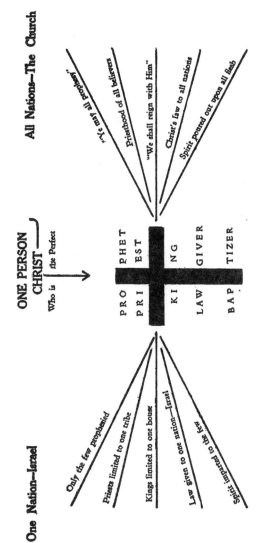

One Nation—Israel

Only the few prophesied
Priests limited to one tribe
Kings limited to one house
Law given to one nation—Israel
Spirit imparted to the few

ONE PERSON CHRIST — Who is { the Perfect

PRO PHET
PRI EST
KI NG
LAW GIVER
BAP TIZER

All Nations—The Church

"Ye may all prophesy"
Priesthood of all believers
"We shall reign with Him"
Christ's law to all nations
Spirit poured out upon all flesh

Figure 4. How the Scriptures Are Fulfilled

ing or testifying to Messiah's finished work is now granted to all, so that we read, "Ye may *all* prophesy one by one." [10]

The priesthood was limited to one tribe, Levi.   Christ, by the sacrifice of Himself, became the one great Priest, who ever lives to make intercession.   Now every believer, whatever his nationality or social status, is call to a priestly ministry, to offer himself as a living sacrifice for service and to offer spiritual sacrifices unto God. [11]

In Old Testament times the divinely chosen king came from one family, the house of David. [12]   Then Jesus appeared of the seed of David according to the flesh, the perfect and eternal King of whom David was but a type. [13] Now, the great King offers to "who-

---

that whosoever will not hearken unto my words which he shall speak in my name, I will require it of him.

Heb. 1:1, 2.—1 God, who at sundry times and in divers manners spake in time past unto the fathers by the prophets,   2 Hath in these last days spoken unto us by his Son,
. . . "

(10) I Cor. 14:31.

(11) Rom. 12:1.—1 I beseech you therefore, brethren, by the mercies of God, that ye present your bodies a living sacrifice, holy, acceptable unto God, which is you reasonable service.

I Peter 2:5.—5 Ye also, as lively stones, are built up a spiritual house, an holy priesthood, to offer up spiritual sacrifices, acceptable to God by Jesus Christ.

(12) Psa. 132:11, 12.—11 The Lord hath sworn in truth unto David; he will not turn from it; Of the fruit of thy body will I set upon thy throne.   12 If thy children will keep my covenant and my testimony that I shall teach them their children shall also sit upon thy throne for evermore.

(13) Rom. 1:3.—3 Concerning his Son Jesus Christ our Lord, which was made of the seed of David according to the flesh.

soever will" the honor of reigning with Him,[14] of sitting on His throne [15] during that period when He shall take full possession of His kingdom.[16]   The offer is "to him that over-cometh."

In those days the Spirit was imparted to the few, to prophets, priests, kings, judges, and others occupying official positions. Jesus came, and upon Him the Spirit descended and *remained;*[17] to Him the Spirit was given without measure [18] and He ministered under a continual anointing.[19]   This Christ, this perfectly anointed One, now baptizes in the Holy Ghost "whosoever will," and in relation to this anointing there is neither Jew nor

Luke 1:32, 33.—32 He shall be great, and shall be called the Son of the Highest: and the Lord God shall give unto him the throne of his father David: 33 And he shall reign over the house of Jacob for ever; and of his kingdom there shall be no end.

(14) 2 Tim. 2:12.—12 If we suffer, we shall also reign with him: if we deny him, he also will deny us.

(15) Rev. 3:21.—21 To him that overcometh will I grant to sit with me in my throne, even as I also overcame, and am set down with my Father in his throne.

(16) Rev. 20:6.—6 Blessed and holy is he that hath part in the first resurrection: on such the second death hath no power, but they shall be priests of God and of Christ, and shall reign with him a thousand years.

(17) John 1:33.—33 And I knew him not: but he that sent me to baptize with water, the same said to me, Upon whom thou shalt see the Spirit descending, and remaining on him, the same is he which baptizeth with the Holy Ghost.

(18) John 3:34.—34 For he whom God hath sent speaketh the words of God: for God giveth not the Spirit by measure unto him.

(19) Acts 10:38.—38 How God anointed Jesus of Nazareth with the Holy Ghost, and with power: who went about doing good, and healing all that were oppressed of the devil; for God was with him.

Greek, there is neither bond nor free, there is neither male nor female. "For the promise is unto you, and to your children, and to all that are afar off, even as many as the Lord our God shall call."[20]

The Law was given to one nation, Israel, who guarded it with a jealous exclusiveness. Jesus, the perfect lawgiver, gave the true interpretation and spiritual meaning of the law[21] and died and rose that all might have the power to keep it. Then after His resurrection He commanded that *His* law be given to *all nations.*[22]

Thus Christ fulfills the Scriptures. All the blessings of the Old Testament, once limited to one nation, one tribe, one family, or to certain favored individuals, now become available to "whosoever will" by the work of the great Fulfiller, who has become the distributing agent for that great store of ancient treasure, and who is ready to open wide His hands and enrich all who, in poverty of spirit, seek the true riches.

---

(20) Acts 2:39.

(21) Matt. chs. 5-7.

(22) Matt. 28:19-20.—19 Go ye therefore, and teach all nations, baptizing them in the name of the Father, and of the Son, and of the Holy Ghost: 20 Teaching them to observe all things whatsoever I have commanded you: and, lo, I am with you alway even unto the end of the world. Amen.

John 13:34.—34 A new commandment I give unto you, That ye love one another; as I have loved you, that ye also love one another.

Gal. 6:2.—2 Bear ye one another's burdens, and so fulfil the law of Christ.

II

The Plan in the Book of Genesis

Having learned that the Bible has one predominant theme, the redemption of the race, we shall now trace that theme through the different divisions of the Scriptures. We shall note how in divers manners and through many instruments and channels, God fulfilled His great purpose throughout all the checkered history of Israel, His chosen people; how, in spite of apostasy and human failure and through the severest of judgments, He made all things work together for good for the accomplishment of His plan.

This plan we shall study in the book of Genesis, which tells the story of (1) *Generation:* or how the stage for the drama of redemption was created, together with those who were to become the beneficiaries of that redemption; (2) *Degeneration:* how mankind fell into a condition that made redemption necessary; (3) *Regeneration:* how God chose an individual, a family, a nation through whom to accomplish that redemption.

There are many stories in the book of Genesis. Here is *the* story:

The account of the Creation in which we see *man as God intended him to be,* made in His image, walking in unbroken fellowship with Him, and ruling the world with God-given power.

The account of the Fall, in which we learn *how man became as he now is.* Yielding to the tempter by an act of his own will, he brings upon himself and his posterity the penalty of sin, death.

A gleam of hope shines through the darkness of the curse—the bright promise of *redemption.*[1] This scripture predicts a constant struggle between humanity and the power that caused its fall, resulting in a victory for humanity, through suffering. This promise was fulfilled through mankind's representative, *the Son of man,* who went about doing good and healing all that were oppressed of the devil, whom He defeated through His atoning sufferings and death.[2]

Of Adam's sons, *Seth* is chosen as the one through whom the Redeemer shall come. Eve recognizes this fact for she says, "The Lord hath appointed me another seed.[3]

From this time on two classes of people, the godly Sethites and the ungodly Cainites,

---

(1) Gen. 3:15.—15 And I will put enmity between thee and the woman, and between thy seed and her seed; it shall bruise thy head, and thou shalt bruise his heel.

(2) I John 3:8.—8 He that committeth sin is of the devil; for the devil sinneth from the beginning. For this purpose the Son of God was manifested, that he might destroy the works of the devil.

(3) Gen. 4:25.

come into prominence. As time passes the line of separation between these is obliterated, and finally the race drifts into that state of corruption which brings on the Flood. Of Seth's descendants *Noah* is chosen as the one who shall become the channel of the world's redemption.

After the Flood the earth is repeopled by the descendants of Noah's three sons, Shem, Ham, and Japheth. Of these *Shem* is chosen as the father of the race to whom God will reveal Himself in an especial way.[4]

So far we have been dealing with the *introduction* to the book of Genesis, and also to the Bible itself. The eleven chapters constituting this introduction deal with the history of the *race* showing how conditions arose that made world-salvation necessary. The chapters that follow describe God's dealings with a chosen individual from whom is to come a chosen family which will finally grow into a chosen nation. In a sense, the history of the Bible really begins with *Abraham,* the father of the Hebrew people. To him the gospel was first proclaimed; in the words of Paul, "And the scripture foreseeing that God would justify the heathen through faith, preached before the gospel unto Abraham saying, In thee shall all nations be blessed."[5] To the New Testament writers this is *the*

(4) Gen. 9:26.—26 And he said, Blessed be the Lord God of Shem; and Canaan shall be his servant.
(5) Gal. 3:8.

promise,[6] of which the New Testament is the unfolding. With this promise is connected the outpouring of the Spirit on the Gentiles.[7] This is the promise which anticipates Matthew 28:19, 20 and Acts 1:8,[8] the promise of which the Acts is one great fulfillment. It is this promise whose fulfillment in our own days is being advanced by every missionary of the Cross. *"And in thee shall the families of the earth be blessed."*

Of Abraham's two sons, *Isaac,* the child of promise, is chosen, and to him the promise is renewed.

Of Isaac's two sons, *Jacob,* the God-wrestler, is chosen. To him are born twelve sons who become the fathers of the twelve tribes of *the nation of Israel.*

Of these tribes *Judah* is chosen as the tribe

---

(6) Acts 13:23, 32, 33.—23 Of this man's seed hath God according to his promise raised unto Israel a Saviour, Jesus: 32 And we declare unto you glad tidings, how that the promise which was made unto the fathers, 33 God hath fulfilled the same unto us their children, in that he hath raised up Jesus again; as it is also written in the second psalm, Thou art my Son, this day have I begotten thee.

(7) Gal. 3:14.—14 That the blessing of Abraham might come on the Gentiles through Jesus Christ; that we might receive the promise of the Spirit through faith.

Acts 10:45.—45 And they of the circumcision which believed were astonished, as many as came with Peter, because that on the Gentiles also was poured out the gift of the Holy Ghost.

Acts 15:8, 9.—8 And God, which knoweth the hearts, bare them witness, giving them the Holy Ghost, even as he did unto us; 9 And put no difference between us and them, purifying their hearts by faith.

(8) Matt. 28:19, 20.—19 Go ye therefore, and teach all nations, baptizing them in the name of the Father, and of the Son, and of the Holy Ghost: 20 Teaching them to ob-

from which shall come the great Ruler and the Gatherer of the nations.[9]

Two more prominent names from other sections of the Bible complete the plan. From the tribe of Judah comes *David*, who receives the promise that his throne shall be occupied by the Messiah-King.[10] From the house of David comes *Jesus*, concerning whom it was said that He should be given the throne of David, reign over the house of Jacob forever, and save His people from their sins.[11]

Consult Figure 5 on page 30. The arrow represents the line of redemption. It begins with the first promise of redemption in Gen. 3:15, and ends with its fulfillment in Christ. Between a missionary's promise to visit a country and his arrival, there intervene journeys through different countries in various modes of transportation, and the many experiences

---

serve all things whatsoever I have commanded you: and, lo, I am with you alway, even unto the end of the world. Amen.

Acts 1:8.—8 But ye shall receive power, after that the Holy Ghost is come upon you: and ye shall be witnesses unto me both in Jerusalem, and in all Judæa, and in Samaria, and unto the uttermost part of the earth.

(9) Gen. 49:10.—10 The sceptre shall not depart from Judah, nor a lawgiver from between his feet, until Shiloh come; and unto him shall the gathering of the people be.

(10) Read 2 Sam. 7 and Psa. 72.

(11) Luke 1:32, 33.—32 He shall be great, and shall be called the Son of the Highest: and the Lord God shall give unto him the throne of his father David: 33 And he shall reign over the house of Jacob for ever; and of his kingdom there shall be no end.

Matt. 1:21.—21 And she shall bring forth a son, and thou shalt call his name Jesus; for he shall save his people from their sins.

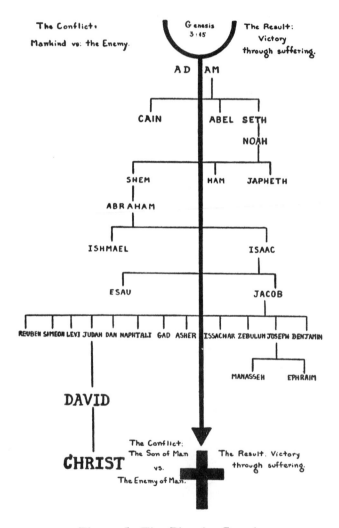

Figure 5. The Plan in Genesis.

incidental to a long voyage. So it was between the promise of redemption and its arrival to the race in the person of Christ. The names on the chart represent the various channels through which the promise came, and the many events and experiences connected with those names.

III

The Birth and Education of a Nation

(Exodus to Deuteronomy)

The Book of Genesis concludes with the account of the descent of the chosen family into Egypt to escape the famine in Canaan. In this connection it should be noted that the beautiful story of Joseph was not written to entertain, nor even *primarily* to impart the moral lessons which it contains, but to indicate the part Joseph played in God's plan of redemption—to preserve the chosen family from which the chosen nation was to come.[1]

BIRTH PAINS

Israel's bitter experience of bondage was not a failure in the divine plan, but rather a part of it. For, consider how that experience prepared the Israelitish nation for their great mission:

The fire of suffering welded the nation into a real unity based upon a common experience. Such has been the effect of tribula-

---

(1) Gen. 45:7.—7 And God sent me before you to preserve you a posterity in the earth, and to save your lives by a great deliverance.

Gen. 50:20.—20 But as for you, ye thought evil against me; but God meant it unto good, to bring to pass, as it is this day, to save much people alive.

tion upon this nation throughout its history. A few years ago a prominent manufacturer launched an attack against the Jews in which he accused their leaders of engineering a plot that would harm, in some way, the Gentile world. During the period of this anti-Semitic propaganda it was observed that the attendance and membership in the synagogues and Jewish fraternal organizations rose to a higher point than that attained in times of security. While the real object of the attack was the Jewish capitalist, yet the unity of the nation was such that, as someone humorously observed, "If the face of one Jew were struck, the nose of the entire nation would bleed!"

It kept the nation separated. If the Israelites had been permitted to prosper in Egypt how vain would have been the attempt to inspire them with a love for Canaan, especially when a long journey through appalling dangers and formidable difficulties was involved. For them it was best that they enter the kingdom through much tribulation.

Their experience did for them what conviction for sin accomplishes for a person in this dispensation—it caused them to feel their need of deliverance and to call upon the God who was only too ready and willing to save them.[2] This purpose will become more evi-

(2) Ex. 2:23-25.—23 And it came to pass in progress of time, that the king of Egypt died: and the children of Israel sighed by reason of the bondage, and they cried, and

dent if we may consider (as a noted scholar has suggested) that the Egyptian bondage was a judgment upon the Israelites for falling into Egyptian idolatry and corruption and forgetting the covenant made with their fathers.[3]

Their experience prepared them for a new revelation of God—as *Jehovah their Saviour*. In later ages, when they were oppressed by Gentile powers, their deliverance from Egypt by the mighty outstretched hand of Jehovah became to them a measure of God's power.

Their bondage served a practical purpose in relation to their civilization.   It was for the nation a time of education in practical matters, a time of learning habits of labor and industry. When they entered Canaan they were equipped with a knowledge of art and manufactures and with a capacity for active business and employment.

CHOSEN TO SERVE

Why was *Israel* chosen as God's own people? Certainly not because of any favoritism

their cry came up unto God by reason of the bondage.   24 And God heard their groaning, and God remembered his covenant with Abraham, with Isaac, and with Jacob.   25 And God looked upon the children of Israel, and God had respect unto them.

(3) Josh. 24:14.—14 Now therefore fear the Lord, and serve him in sincerity and in truth: and put away the gods which your fathers served on the other side of the flood, and in Egypt; and serve ye the Lord.

Ezek. 23:3.—3 And they committed whoredoms in Egypt; they committed whoredoms in their youth: there were their breasts pressed, and there they bruised the teats of their virginity.

on the Lord's part. A rich man once visited a mountain region where he became acquainted with an illiterate mountain boy who was working for a harsh employer. His attachment for the boy became so strong that he chose him to be his adopted son. He separated him from the rest of the mountain folk, took him to his own home and there educated him, instructing him in religious, moral and practical subjects. His purpose in choosing this particular individual was that, after the boy's training he might return to instruct and elevate his own people. So then, in choosing this one young man the rich man was prompted by love for *all* the mountain people. After the boy's preparation was completed his benefactor sent him to the mountains, with a warning against participating in the sins of the mountaineers and marrying one who was not of his faith.

However instead of busying himself with the task of educating and lifting his fellows, the young man became proud, considered himself superior to other people, and despised them. They returned his scorn with hatred, so that a wall of enmity was raised between him and his fellows. The rich man, hearing of the situation, sent his own son with a message of warning. Dressed in the simple clothes of the mountaineer, as a rebuke to the exclusiveness of the adopted son, the rich man's own son brought a message of tender entreaty from his father. But blinded by pride, the young mountaineer rejected his message, murdered him and fled as an outlaw.

This is not a true story, but a parable, illustrating Israel's history from their departure from Egypt to their rejection of Christ. The rich man represents the God of Israel; the adopted son, Israel; the natural son, Christ. Jehovah saw Israel under the power of a cruel tyrant, Pharaoh, king of Egypt. He loved the nation,[4] delivered them, separated them from all other peoples,[5] chose them to be His adopted son,[6] and took them through a process of national education. His purpose in so favoring this nation was that they might be the means of enlightening and elevating the other nations.[7] But Israel became proud and self-righteous, despised the Gentiles and incurred their enmity. When God's own Son came with a message of warning, Israel rejected Him and caused Him to be crucified. As a penalty they became wanderers among all nations.

---

(4) Deut. 7:8.—8 But because the Lord loved you, and because he would keep the oath which he had sworn unto your fathers, hath the Lord brought you out with a mighty hand, and redeemed you out of the house of bondmen, from the hand of Pharaoh king of Egypt.

(5) Deut. 7:6.—6 For thou art an holy people unto the Lord thy God: the Lord thy God hath chosen thee to be a special people unto himself, above all people that are upon the face of the earth.

(6) Ex. 4:22.—22 And thou shalt say unto Pharaoh, Thus saith the Lord, Israel is my son, even my firstborn:

(7) Compare Gen. 12:2,3.—2 And I will make of thee a great nation, and I will bless thee, and make thy name great; and thou shalt be a blessing: 3 And I will bless

In this chapter we are especially concerned with that part of the story which deals with the choosing of the young man.   The lesson conveyed is that *Israel was chosen to serve.* They were the priest-nation set apart *from* the other nations, to minister *to* all peoples. In lighting a fire we begin with one faggot; when the Lord of the whole earth purposed to enflame the whole world with the holy fire of divine truth He must needs begin with one nation.   Since it was the mission of this nation to be the channel for the development and proclamation of the one true world religion, God, through His dealings with them, made them specialists in divine truth; for specialization is necessary to efficiency in any sphere of activity.   Jesus had reference to this truth when He said, "Salvation is of the Jews";[8] also Paul, when he described the privileges of the chosen people in these words, "Who are Israelites; to whom pertaineth the adoption, and the glory, and the covenants, and the giving of the law, and the service of God, and the promises; whose are the fathers, and of whom, as concerning the flesh Christ came, who is over all, God blessed forever. Amen." [9]   These favors and privileges were conferred upon Israel, not that they should

---

them that bless thee, and curse him that curseth thee: and in thee shall all families of the earth be blessed.

Ex. 19:6.—6 And ye shall be unto me a kingdom of priests, and an holy nation.

(8) John 4:22.

(9) Rom. 9:4, 5.

be ministered unto, but that they should minister, and be so used by God that the blessing of Abraham might come upon all nations.

THE ORGANIZATION OF A NATION

After a series of practical lessons in the walk of faith, Israel arrived at Mount Sinai where they were formally organized as a nation and granted a constitution, generally known as the Law. The Law consisted of three divisions: the moral law, or the Ten Commandments; the civil law, which applied the ten commandments to the everyday life of the people; the ceremonial law, which made provision for Israel's worship, and for their forgiveness in case of violation of any law. The most important section, the foundation of all laws, the very heart of the Old Covenant was the Ten Commandments, "that grand expression of God's holiness, and summary of man's duty, comprehending all that a divinely called people as well as any single individual should do in reference to God and their neighbor." They were *ten* in number, to express their divine perfection; they were written on tables of *stone* to signify their perpetuity; they were written on *both sides* of the tablets, as if to testify that nothing was to be added.

"How can two walk together except they be agreed?" [10] The Law provided a basis of

_____

(10) Amos 3:3.

fellowship between Jehovah and His people. It was a revelation to Israel of the kind of conduct Jehovah required from a redeemed people who were to enter upon a world-wide mission. It formed a bond of union between the Lord and His people, for by obeying the Law Israel would retain Jehovah's presence with them, and God and people would dwell together in the national home, Canaan. In connection with this thought it is interesting to note that the prophets often described Jehovah's relationship to His people as that of husband to wife.[11] The marriage ceremony, so to speak, was performed at Sinai. Moses was the mediator.[12] Jehovah vowed faithfulness and promised to be their God;[13] the people, on their part, promised to be faithful to Jehovah.[14] The seal of his union was sacrificial blood.[15] In later times Israel's vio-

---

(11) Read Hosea chapters 1 to 3.

(12) Ex. 19:17.—17 And Moses brought forth the people out of the camp to meet with God; and they stood at the nether part of the mount.

(13) Ex. 19:5.—5 Now therefore, if ye will obey my voice indeed, and keep my covenant, then ye shall be a peculiar treasure unto me above all people: for all the earth is mine.

(14) Ex. 19:8.—8 And all the people answered together, and said, All that the Lord hath spoken we will do. And Moses returned the words of the people unto the Lord.

(15) Ex. 24:5-8.—5 And he sent young men of the children of Israel, which offered burnt offerings, and sacrificed peace offerings of oxen unto the Lord. 6 And Moses took half of the blood, and put it in basons; and half of the blood he sprinkled on the altar. 7 And he took the book of the covenant, and read in the audience of the people: and they said, All that the Lord hath said will we do, and be obedient. 8 And Moses took the blood, and sprinkled it on the people, and said, Behold the blood of the covenant,

lation of the law and their worshipping of idols was denounced as the sin of adultery, the violation of the marriage vow.

The law served a very important purpose in the divine plan of redemption which is the main theme of our study. As the people attempted to live up to its high standard many of them became painfully conscious of the existence of a sinful nature that made impossible a perfect heart-felt conformity to the divine will. In the Book of Psalms, the book of Israel's experience, we hear earnest petitions for the grace and power of God to tranform sinful hearts.[16] Thus the law became a schoolmaster to lead Israelitish saints to Christ,[17] who was to die to deliver them from its penalty,[18] and who was to change their sinful hearts,[19] by writing the law thereon with the Spirit of God.[20]

---

which the Lord hath made with you concerning all these words.

(16) Read for example, Psalm 51.

(17) Gal. 3:24.—24 Wherefore the law was our schoolmaster to bring us unto Christ, that we might be justified by faith.

(18) Gal. 3:13.—13 Christ hath redeemed us from the curse of the law, being made a curse for us: for it is written, Cursed is every one that hangeth on a tree.

(19) II Cor. 5:17.—17 Therefore if any man be in Christ, he is a new creature: old things are passed away; behold, all things are become new.

(20) Jer. 31:31-33.—31 Behold, the days come, saith the Lord, that I will make a new covenant with the house of Israel, and with the house of Judah: 32 Not according to the covenant that I made with their fathers in the day that I took them by the hand to bring them out of the land of Egypt; which my covenant they brake, although I was an husband unto them, saith the Lord: 33 But this shall be the covenant that I will make with the house of

THE PALACE OF THE GREAT KING

Having become united to Israel in the bonds of holy covenant relations, Jehovah desired to make an arrangement whereby He could dwell with them, so that there should be a definite place where they could always find Him "at home," and so approach Him to obtain mercy and find grace to help in time of need. To accomplish this purpose He commanded the construction of the Tabernacle. Let us consider this sanctuary from three different viewpoints:

Jehovah's Palace

Israel was a theocracy, that is, a state whose ruler is God. Since Jehovah was King of Israel,[21] and the Tabernacle was His dwelling place,[22] it will be legitimate to look upon the Tabernacle as the palace of Jehovah. In the Holy of Holies, His throne room, He is enthroned above the ark,[23] which contains the Law, the constitution of His kingdom. In the Holy Place, the priests, His ministers of state, serve Him and from there go forth to

Israel; After those days, saith the Lord, I will put my law in their inward parts, and write it in their hearts; and will be their God, and they shall be my people.

(21) I Sam. 12:12.—12 And when ye saw that Nahash the king of the children of Ammon came against you, ye said unto me, Nay; but a king shall reign over us: when the Lord your God was your king.

(22) Ex. 25:8.—8 And let them make me a sanctuary; that I may dwell among them.

(23) Ex. 25:22.—22 And there I will meet with thee, and I will commune with thee from above the mercy seat, from between the two cherubims which are upon the ark of the testimony, of all things which I will give thee in commandment unto the children of Israel.

teach His laws to the people.   Into the court
come the subjects of the King, bringing gifts
as an expression of their gratitude and loyal-
ty, and sacrifices, as a confession that they
have violated His laws and need His forgiveness.   It is at the Tabernacle that He must
be consulted on all matters which concern the
welfare of His people.

To a limited extent a person's character
may be judged by the condition and furnish-
ings of his home; its cleanliness, the pictures
on the wall, the type of furniture used, the
contents of the bookcase—all tell us something of the one who lives in the home.   In
like manner we shall learn of the great King's
character by studying His dwelling.   Let us
imagine the palace of an earthly king, built
in such a way as to be an expression of the
king's character, a palace where every piece of
furniture and every apartment express in
symbolic form the king's attitude toward his
subjects and his plans for their present and
future welfare.   This will illustrate the purpose of the Tabernacle which was a symboli-
cal and typical expression of the character,
will, and purpose of Jehovah, arranged to
teach: (1) The holiness of the King; (2)
The sinfulness and inward rebelliousness of
His subjects; (3) His plan for so transform-
ing the lives of His subjects that they will
serve Him out of pure love.

The A. B. C. of the Plan of Redemption

We may consider the Tabernacle as a divinely appointed series of pictorial illustrations whereby a nation of spiritual children studied the A. B. C. of the plan of redemption, in anticipation of their graduation through a definite experience with the Christ.[24] As God has used symbols of Nature to show forth the coming of the Redeemer (e. g., *sun* of righteousness, *root* of David, the *branch,* the *lamb,* the *lion* of Judah), so in the Tabernacle He employed different articles of furniture, and objects connected with worship, as foreshadowing illustrations of the perfect salvation to come.

As the Israelite observed the white curtain surrounding the tabernacle, he was made to feel that his sinfulness excluded him from God's presence, but he was glad to see one door, that gave him access. Facing him was the great brazen altar which spoke to him of pardon for the sin that excluded him. As he watched his representative, the priest, wash in the laver before entering the Holy Place, he learned that purity was necessary to divine service. As the priest trimmed the great seven-branch lamp, he learned the truth of spiritual illumination. The table with the twelve loaves of shewbread spoke of the divine provision for spiritual nourishment. The golden altar of incense before the vail testified to the power and preciousness of in-

(24) Read Gal. 3:24 to 4:7.

tercession before God.   No farther could the
priest go, for the vail before the Holy of
Holies taught that perfect access to God was
not possible as yet.   However on the Day of
Atonement, as the high priest, representing
the people, entered that mysterious shrine to
sprinkle the mercy seat with atoning blood,
the discerning Israelite would be encouraged
to believe in a coming day when perfect atonement would be made.

But mankind could not forever study the
A. B. C., the elements of the plan of redemption.   The blood of bulls and goats could
not give permanent relief for the conscience,
the laver could not yield the true spiritual
cleansing, the golden lampstand was not able
to illuminate the millions of darkened hearts,
the shewbread could not feed the multitude,
the golden altar could not rend the heavens
that perfect salvation might come.   These
things were but the shadow that testified to
the presence and coming of the reality.   So
in about a generation after the Lamb of God
had made atonement, after the Light of the
world had manifested Himself, and the Bread
of life had declared Himself, and the High
Priest and Sanctifier had ascended to the very
Holy of Holies in heaven itself—after all these
things had come to pass, the Temple (representing the Tabernacle in permanent form)
passed away.   It had performed its divinely
appointed task of educating mankind in those
truths which were fulfilled by the Lord Jesus

Christ. For us it must now decrease in order that He might increase. Yet it will be to us as a precious goblet that brought to us the life-giving draft of the healing waters of divine truth, it will be useful to us as a constant reminder of Him who is Truth incarnate.

An Advance Step in the Plan of Redemption

The Tabernacle represents an advance step in God's revelation of His plan of redemption. Observe Figure 6 on page 46. The Cross was eternally in God's heart and mind in heaven, before it was ever manifested on earth.[25] After man's fall, the appeal of human need called forth the manifestation of the Cross in human history, The truth of the atonement, symbolized by the cross, was first revealed through the institution of the altar, the worshiping place of the patriarchs. Then through the Tabernacle and Temple the plan of salvation was revealed more completely. Finally, at the crucifixion of the Saviour, the cross that had been in the mind and heart of God before the foundation of the world was set up at Calvary. Instead of an altar was a rude Roman cross; instead of a lamb, the Son of God Himself. After His atoning work, our Lord rose and ascended to the

---

(25) I Peter 1:19, 20.—19 But with the precious blood of Christ, as of a lamb without blemish and without spot: 20 Who verily was foreordained before the foundation of the world, but was manifest in these last times for you.

Rev. 13:8.—8 And all that dwell upon the earth shall worship him, whose names are not written in the book of life of the Lamb slain from the foundation of the world.

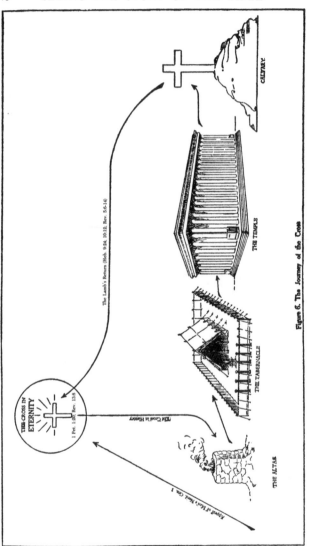

Figure 6. The Journey of the Cross

Father, there to continue His priestly work for us and in a future day to receive the worship of the heavenly hosts, the redeemed, and all creation, who will sing, "Worthy is the Lamb that was slain to receive power and riches, and wisdom, and strength and glory and honor and blessing."

SACRED ETIQUETTE

Before persons are presented before the king and queen of England, they are carefully and minutely instructed as to the proper dress to wear, the manner of greeting the monarchs, the words to be spoken; in short, they are carefully drilled in court etiquette. It is considered necessary and fitting that those representing the dignity and power of a great empire should be approached with respect and reverence. So Jehovah, the ruler of the whole earth, laid down rules to be followed by those who desired to approach Him. He would teach His people at the very beginning of their national life that He is the great King, high and lifted up, who will not tolerate the familiarity that breeds contempt. These rules are found in Leviticus, the Old Testament book of sacred ritual, and may be summed up as follows: (1) The sacrifices taught the people that without the shedding of atoning blood, for the covering of sin, there could be no access to Jehovah. (2) The commands relating to the bathing of the flesh and washing of garments taught them that a holy God requires a holy people. "Ye shall

be holy, for I the Lord your God am holy." [26]
(3) The institution of the priesthood conveyed the lesson that the people were unworthy to approach the King directly, but
were in need of mediators and intercessors.

While the rules of the book of Leviticus
are not binding on Christians, the New Testament contains suggestions of a spiritual etiquette, that would teach us not to enter rash-
ly and unprepared into the presence of the
Lord of lords.

APPROACHING THE PROMISED LAND

In our introductory chapter we noticed
that God's great plan of redemption as recorded in the Scriptures was not thwarted
by human failure. The book of Numbers
contains an outstanding illustration of this
principle.[27]   Redeemed from Egypt by a
mighty manifestation of divine power, given
many evidences of God's presence with them,
and constituted God's own people, Israel
came to Kadesh Barnea, the place of opportunity, and the point from which they were
to march directly into Canaan. The story
of their failure and punishment is familiar.
Jehovah's plan may be delayed, but it is not
defeated by Israel's failure, for He says, "as
truly as I live, all the earth shall be filled with
the glory of the Lord." [28]   In like manner,
in spite of Israel's failure at Calvary, the place

(26) Lev. 19:2.
(27) Read Num. 14.
(28) Num. 14:21.

of their national crisis,[29] the whole world
has been filled with the glory of the Lord,
for through Israel's fall salvation has come
to the Gentiles; and as He has visited the
Gentiles, so He will again visit His own in
the last days.[30]   Paul, seeing the wisdom of
the Divine plan that cannot be defeated by
human failure, bursts forth into song; "O
the depth of the riches both of the wisdom
and knowledge of God! how unsearchable
are his judgments, and his ways past finding
out! . . . For of Him, and through him,
and to him are all things: to whom be glory
forever." [31]

The death of God's servants does not cause
His plan to halt.   The Book of Deuteronomy
records the farewell discourses and the death
of Moses.   The worker passes on, but the
work continues; the instrument serves out
his time of usefulness, but the Divine Worker

---

(29) Luke 19:41-44.—41 And when he was come near, he
beheld the city, and wept over it, 42 Saying, If thou hadst
known, even thou, at least in this thy day, the things which
belong unto thy peace! but now they are hid from thine
eye. 43 For the days shall come upon thee, that thine enemies shall cast a trench about thee, and compass thee
round, and keep thee in on every side, 44 And shall lay
thee even with the ground, and thy children within thee;
and they shall not leave in thee one stone upon another;
because thou knewest not the time of thy visitation.

(30) Rom. 11:11, 12.—11 I say then, Have they stumbled
that they should fall? God forbid: but rather through their
fall salvation is come unto the Gentiles, for to provoke them
to jealousy. 12 Now if the fall of them be the riches of the
world, and the diminishing of them the riches of the Gentiles; how much more their fulness?

(31) Rom. 11:33, 36.

finds others.   Whenever a Moses dies, God
has a Joshua to take his place and to carry on
the divine work.

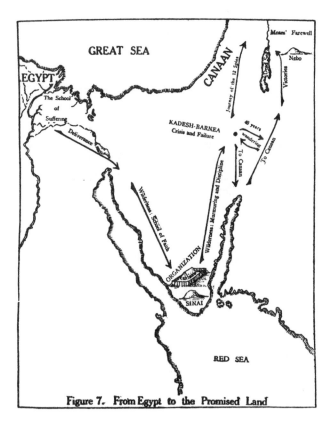

Figure 7. From Egypt to the Promised Land

BIRTH AND EDUCATION OF A NATION: OUTLINE OF THE HISTORY

EGYPT: ISRAEL IN THE SCHOOL OF SUFFERING.

1. The experience of suffering unites the tribes.
2. It keeps them separated.
3. Makes them feel their need of God.
4. Prepares them for a new revelation of God.
5. They receive practical training.

DELIVERANCE: THE BIRTH OF A NATION.

1. The birth, training and call of Moses.
2. The plagues. Israel delivered by God's power.
3. The Passover. Israel sheltered under atoning blood.
4. Baptism in Red Sea (1 Cor. 10:1, 2); beginning of a new life.

THE WILDERNESS: ISRAEL IN SCHOOL OF FAITH.

1. Wilderness food: manna.
2. Wilderness refreshment: water from rock.
3. Wilderness guidance: pillar of fire and cloud.
4. Wilderness victory: Amalek defeated.

SINAI: ISRAEL ORGANIZED.

1. The law covenant.
2. Israel in the school of redemption: erection of tabernacle.

   3. Israel in school of holiness: laws of Leviticus.

   4. Numbering and organization.

TO KADESH BARNEA: THE CRISIS.

   1. In the wilderness: murmurings, rebellions and punishments.

   2. The Great Refusal: Israel discouraged by spies.

   3. The penalty: forty years of national death.

THE NEW GENERATION ON THE WAY TO CANAAN.

   1. Moses' sin.   A new leader appointed for the new generation.

   2. Aaron's death.   New high priest appointed for the new generation.

   3. Murmurings, punishments, victories.

   4. At borders of Canaan.   Moses dies, Joshua takes command.

Isolation and Dispersion

(Joshua to Esther)

From now on we shall notice two stages in God's preparation of His people for their world-wide mission of bringing to all nations the knowledge of the one true God and His plan of redemption. The two stages are: A period of isolation when the Israelites were separated from other nations; and a period of dispersion, when they mingled freely with other nations.

ISRAEL'S ISOLATION (JOSHUA TO CHRONI-CLES)

During this period Israel was located in one land, educated by the laws and institutions given through Moses, and through the ministry of the prophets inspired with the hope of God's coming kingdom. Before permitting them to mingle freely with all nations for their national ministry of witnessing to the true God and His word, the Lord, through His dealing with Israel, placed a stamp upon the character of the nation that forever made them different from all other peoples. Let us notice the different stages in Israel's separation.

Their settlement in Canaan. The Lord had promised Abraham that through his descendants all nations would be blessed; his descendants would later form a *nation* that would be the channel of this redemption; and to this nation, a *land* would be given, in which they should prepare for their great mission. This was the land of Canaan, which was to become the scene of Jehovah's manifestation of Himself and the stage on which the events were to take place which would reveal His glory and salvation to all the earth. The book of Joshua tells us how the nation took possession of their new home. Jehovah was the Lord of the land. The tenants before Israel had polluted His property.[1] Therefore the Lord of the land commissioned Israel to expel the unworthy tenants and take possession. The land was not really Israel's, but was leased to them [2] under certain conditions.[3] Violation of these conditions would result in their expulsion.

The Law. The Mosaic ritual and the whole system of Judaism was developed and

(1) Gen. 15:16.—16 But in the fourth generation they shall come hither again: for the iniquity of the Amorites is not yet full.

Lev. 18:24, 25.—24 Defile not ye yourselves in any of these things: for in all these the nations are defiled which I cast out before you: 25 And the land is defiled: therefore I do visit the iniquity thereof upon it, and the land itself vomiteth out her inhabitants.

(2) Lev. 25:23.—23 The land shall not be sold for ever: for the land is mine; for ye are strangers and sojourners with me.

(3) Read Lev. 26 and Deut. 28.

perfected in the land of promise, and reached the height of its glory during the reign of Solomon. That the law of Moses did keep the people separate is well illustrated by Peter's experience.[4]

The ministry of the prophets. While the ministry of the priesthood helped to keep the people separated from the nations, the ministry of the prophets, generally speaking, was to keep before the people the *purpose* of this separation.[5]

During times of national apostasy the prophets kept alive the flame of vital religion.[6] In times of national distress they encouraged the faithful with the hope of the coming of Messiah, who would bring everlasting redemption. The working of God's Spirit through the prophets made an impression upon Israel's character that rendered

(4) Acts 10:28.—28 And he said unto them, Ye know how that it is an unlawful thing for a man that is a Jew to keep company, or come unto one of another nation; but God hath shewed me that I should not call any man common or unclean.

(5) Isa. 43:10-12.—10 Ye are my witnesses, saith the Lord, and my servant whom I have chosen: that ye may know and believe me, and understand that I am he: before me there was no God formed, neither shall there be after me. 11 I, even I, am the Lord; and beside me there is no saviour. 12 I have declared, and have saved, and I have shewed, when there was no strange god among you: therefore ye are my witnesses, saith the Lord, that I am God.

Isa. 60:1-3.—1 Arise, shine; for thy light is come, and the glory of the Lord is risen upon thee. 2 For, behold, the darkness shall cover the earth, and gross darkness the people: but the Lord shall arise upon thee, and his glory shall be seen upon thee. 3 And the Gentiles shall come to thy light, and kings to the brightness of thy rising.

(6) Read I Kings 18.

them different from all other peoples. This is practically admitted by a very modernistic Jewish writer, who attributes the mysterious "something" in the Jew's make-up to the power working through the seers.

ISRAEL'S DISPERSION (EZRA TO ESTHER)

In nature, the period of the dispersion was missionary, divinely intended to prepare the Gentile world for Christ's coming. Though the experience of captivity, resulting in dispersion, followed God's judgments on Israel, and did not represent His best for them, yet it is one of the "all things" that worked together for good in the accomplishing of God's purpose. It is interesting to note that when God would discipline His people in preparation for their world mission, He sent them to the very country where Abraham learned about world redemption—the land of Babylonia. It seems that in order to teach His people a lesson of faith, He sent them to the same heathen surroundings where their father Abraham first learned it.

Let us consider how the experiences referred to prepared Israel for their work.

They returned from Babylon entirely cleansed from idolatry—a necessary transformation for those who were to witness to the unity and spirituality of God. Also, they returned with a wider and deeper knowledge of the nature of God. After the destruction of their temple they learned that the Lord was not limited to any one building, but dwells with him who is of a contrite and humble spirit. When sacrifices ceased for a time they found out that He would accept the sacrifices of sincere devotion and surrendered life.

Contact with foreign peoples broadened their vision so that, very gradually, the truth dawned upon them that they could impart their religion to other peoples. Under the teaching of the prophets, who had taught universal redemption, and whose messages were studied by the exiles, the consciousness deepened within them that they were the Lord's witnesses to the Gentiles, to shine into the darkness of their sin and idolatry.

They returned, no longer a *political* body, but a *religious* company, whose function was to develop a spiritual life based on Moses and the Prophets, and to preserve and give to the world those Scriptures which told of the Redeemer's coming. Jerusalem was restored, not a great national center as under David and Solomon, but as a spiritual headquarters to the scattered nation, and as an "information bureau" for divine truth, to which Gentiles could later come, asking "Where is He that is born King of the Jews?"

As the people felt the weight of Gentile oppression and their own insignificance and weakness, they yearned for the coming of the Messiah who should destroy the oppressor and set up His own kingdom. When the voices of the living prophets were hushed in silence, the Jews pored over their messages, and warmed themselves at the glowing fire of Messianic prophecy, so that when Jesus appeared there was a tense expectation that the Kingdom of the Messiah was near at hand.

After the return those Jews who lived in foreign lands were not able to attend the temple services regularly. Therefore, in order to meet their spiritual needs, and to provide a center of unity for them in the different cities where they lived, synagogues (meeting houses) were organized where prayer was made and the Scriptures read and expounded. The mission of the synagogue in God's purpose was to bring His written word to the Gentile world, and so spread the glad tidings of the coming of the Saviour of all nations. The synagogues made many converts among the Gentiles (called "proselytes" in the New Testament), many of whom were ripe for the gospel when it was first preached.[7] This period witnessed the rise of the scribes, who copied and expounded the Scriptures.

It should be noted that with Israel's increasing outward contact with the Gentiles, there was effected a rigid *inward* separation. This was brought about by Ezra and Nehemiah, the founders of a "holiness movement"

---

(7) Acts 13:43.—43 Now when the congregation was broken up, many of the Jews and religious proselytes followed Paul and Barnabas: who, speaking to them, persuaded them to continue in the grace of God.

based on a strict observance of the law of Moses, and having as its slogan the word "Separation."   In the book of Ezra, chapters 9 and 10, we shall observe an example of the methods of these two zealous reformers.   When Ezra came to Jerusalem he was shocked to find that many of the people were married to heathen wives.   After a time of public mourning and confession he commanded the people to send away their foreign companions.   While this measure may sound harsh to some in these days, yet it saved the nation spiritually by keeping them separate. Without such strict action the Jewish nation would have been like a river without banks that loses itself in swamps and morasses.

With this period the rule of the living *prophets* ends and the rule of the *priests* begins.   Though the latter became formal and lacked the inspiration and power of the prophets, yet they rendered an important service by keeping the law of Moses before the people.   From now on, to speak figuratively, the nation enters a dark tunnel, as far as prophetic inspiration is concerned, and there begins a period of prophetic silence of four hundred years, a silence to be broken at last by the voice of one crying in the wilderness "Repent; for the kingdom of heaven is at hand."

ISOLATION AND DISPERSION: OUTLINE OF THE HISTORY

ISRAEL UNDER THE JUDGES

1. Under Joshua Israel conquers Canaan.
2. Under the judges nation fights as separate tribes. Time of anarchy. A story of sin, servitude, sorrow and salvation.
3. Samuel, last of the judges, unites nation under one king.

THE UNITED KINGDOM

1. The story of Saul the man who lost his crown.
2. The story of David, king, statesman, poet and warrior, who built a great empire.
3. The story of Solomon, whose reign began with brilliance and ended with disaster.

THE DIVIDED KINGDOM

1. The story of Israel. A sad tale of wars, religious conflicts, usurpations and assassination. Elijah, and Elisha, Hosea and Amos preached. The tribes are carried captive to Assyria, and never return as a nation.
2. The story of Judah. The southern kingdom survives the northern by about one hundred years.

    Politically, a story of intrigues,

foreign invasions, foreign alliances, and wars and alliances with the northern kingdom.   Carried captive to Babylon by Nebuchadnezzar.

Religiously, a story of godly and of wicked kings, of apostasies and reformations. Messages of the prophets rejected. Finally after declension and apostasy, comes Divine judgment.

THE CAPTIVITY

1. In Babylon seventy years.
2. Ezekiel and Daniel prophesy.
3. Beginning of dispersion.

THE RETURN

1. Favored by Cyrus king of Persia.
2. Remnant returns under Zerubbabel, the first governor.
3. Temple rebuilt.   Haggai and Zechariah preach.
4. Ezra the scribe, teaches law and promotes a revival of religion.
5. Nehemiah is appointed governor, rebuilds wall and effects reforms.

ISOLATION AND DISPERSION: OUTLINE OF THE PLAN

ISOLATION: ISRAEL LEARNING THE FAITH

1. Establishment in Canaan, as a training school for a world-wide mission.
2. The discipline of the law and ritual: education and separation.

3. The ministry of the prophets, who kept before people their Divine calling.

DISPERSION: ISRAEL PROPAGATING THE FAITH

1. The nation cured of idolatry.
2. Contact with Gentiles broadens their vision.
3. The nation returns, not a political, but a religious group.
4. Under Gentile oppression they yearn for Messiah.
5. Synagogues established, Law and Prophets taught to Gentiles.
6. Rigid separation under Ezra: in the world but not of it.
7. End of prophetic ministry. Priests keep nation separate and scribes preserve the Word.

V

The Heart of the Israelite

(Job to Song of Solomon)

The relation of the poetical books to the other sections of the Old Testament may be explained as follows:

The Historical books tell us about Israel's *deeds*.

The Poetical books tell us about their *feelings*.

The Prophetical books tell about their *preaching*.

These books reveal the emotions and the deepest experiences of the chosen nation as they waited for the manifestation of God's redemption. We hear the response of their hearts to God's dealings with them, and to the experiences, sweet and bitter, that He permitted to come their way. Hence the title of this chapter, "The Heart of the Israelite."

THE BOOK OF JOB

In the course of his experience, the Old Testament saint would notice in the world many things that *seemed* to speak against God's love, justice, and His plan of redemption. The Book of Job deals with one problem that would often perplex him; namely, the question, Why do the righteous suffer? This book was written to teach him that he must not criticize God's ways which are past finding out, but wait in faith until he sees the end of God's dealings with man,[1] and until he sees the whole of the circle of God's plan, of which only a section is now visible. Since an all-wise, all-powerful and all-loving God is on the throne of the universe, all will ultimately be well with His people.

THE PSALMS

The book of Psalms was the great hymn-book of the Jewish nation.   Since hymns grow out of spiritual experience, we shall find here a complete emotional record of the spiritual life of the Old Testament saint covering the whole scale of his experiences with God and man.   It is now *our* hymn book.   The story is told that a great fire swept over a region in Europe, destroying the vineyards and causing what at first seemed an appalling loss.   But the loss really proved to be gain, for the fire had uncovered a vein of silver in the rock.   In like manner the fire of God's Spirit swept over the Old Testament believers, warming, purifying, purging and enlightening.   This fire has left for us a vein of precious metal which we can always mine for the enrichment of our lives.   As Peter was

(1) Jas. 5:11.—11 Behold, we count them happy which endure. Ye have heard of the patience of Job, and have seen the end of the Lord; that the Lord is very pitiful, and of tender mercy.

admonished to strengthen his brethren after his painful experience of denying his Lord, so, in the purpose of God, the varied experiences of these Old Testament believers were recorded for our admonition and comfort.

As we read through the book we discover that we are in the *testimony meeting* of the Old Testament church. They tell us of their experiences of despair, bitter sorrow, spiritual darkness, and moral weakness. But they are careful to say that the Lord delivered them out of all their troubles and imparted to them the joy of His full salvation. *"Deliver"* is one of the great words of this book.

We also find ourselves in the *prayer meeting* of the Old Testament church. While in the Historical books, we hear God talking *about* man, and in the Prophetical books we hear Him talking *to* man, in the Psalms we hear *man talking to God,* pouring out his soul in petition, praise and confession.

Before reading very far we become aware that we are in the midst of a great *song service.* In relation to the plan of redemption, which is our theme, we hear *songs in the night,* uttered when it seemed that God's plan had failed;[2] *coronation songs,* celebrating the appearance of the Messiah-King;[3] *millennial songs,* celebrating the glories of God's coming

---

(2) Read Psa. 89, especially verses 38-52.
(3) Read Psa. 45 and 24.

kingdom.[4]   The book fittingly concludes
with a grand *Hallelujah Chorus,* prophetical
to us of the time when all the saved shall become one mighty choir to sound the praises
of Him who loved us and washed us from
our sins in His own blood.

THE BOOK OF PROVERBS

While waiting for a *future* redemption,
the Israelite was not to become forgetful of
present duties. Therefore, through the gift of
divine wisdom, Solomon and others wrote
the truths contained in the Book of Proverbs,
as heavenly commandments for an earthly
life, as guide posts for the path of everyday
duties.

ECCLESIASTES

In the course of the nation's experience,
many departed from the fear of the Lord
which is the beginning of wisdom, and became skeptical at times in relation to the questions of God's justice and His purposes concerning His creatures. Such an one was the
writer of Ecclesiastes, Solomon, king at Jerusalem. After his lapse, he attempted to find
satisfaction in riches, pleasure, wisdom, and
public achievements. The result of his quest
is expressed in the ever-recurring, melancholy
refrain, "Vanity of vanities; all is vanity."
But the writer finally worked his way
through his moral failures and intellectual

(4) Read **Psa. 72.**

perplexity, and uttered the clear ringing testimony: "Fear God and keep His commandments: for this is the whole duty of man. For God shall bring every work into judgment, with every secret thing, whether it be good or whether it be evil."

THE SONG OF SOLOMON

In this great Melody of Love of the Old Testament we are taught the mutual love of God and His people as typified by the love of bridegroom and bride. This beautiful song testifies that "Many waters cannot quench love, neither can the floods drown it: if a man would give all his substance for love, it would utterly be contemned." [5] This prepares us for that message from the New Testament Song of Songs of brotherly love, "And the greatest of these is love." [6]

---

(5) S. S. 8:17.
(6) I Cor. 13:13.

VI

The Preachers of Israel
(Isaiah to Malachi)

WHO THEY WERE

There is a popular conception of the Hebrew prophet in which he is pictured as an unearthly, mysterious personage, who spends nearly all his time delving into the future. It is true that the prophets predicted future events; but that was only a part of their message, for they had a message that concerned the events of their own day. They were indeed in touch with the great Beyond, yet they were men subject to like passions as we are,[1] ordinary believers, who became extraordinary as they were borne along by God's Spirit.[2] The prophets will become more real and human to us if we describe them as the *Spirit-anointed preachers and evangelists* of Israel.

The nature of the prophetic office will

---

(1) Jas. 5:17.—17 Elias was a man subject to like passions as we are, and he prayed earnestly that it might not rain: and it rained not on the earth by the space of three years and six months.

(2) II Peter 1:21.—21 For the prophecy came not in old time by the will of man: but holy men of God spake as they were moved by the Holy Ghost.

be made clear by contrasting it with the priest-ly office, also divinely ordained.

PRIESTS	PROPHETS
Must belong to the tribe of Levi and be of the male sex.	Could belong to any tribe. Women could prophesy.
Qualifications were prescribed by rigid rules.	Were the free children of the Spirit, whose only qualification was that God's Spirit should be upon them.
Represented the permanency of organized religion.	Represented the divine changing of institutions in order to meet new circumstances.
Were men of the Past, expounding existing revelations.	Were men of the Future, bringing new revelations to meet new conditions, and making new channels for the river of inspiration.
Generally speaking, they represented man before God, and waited for the people to come to them.	Generally speaking, represented God to man, and took the initiative in bringing His message to the people.

WHAT THEY SAW

Observe Figure 8 on page 70. The lower section illustrates what we may call "mountain peaks of prophecy," or prophetic perspective. Let us notice:

The backward look. While the prophets brought new relevations, those revelations were based on promises and covenants proclaimed before their days. The promise of redemption as found in Genesis 3:15 [3] is one of the foundations of their message, for the prophets were heralds of a redemption that

(3) Gen. 3:15.—15 And I will put enmity between thee and the woman, and between thy seed and her seed; it shall **bruise thy head, and thou shalt bruise his heel.**

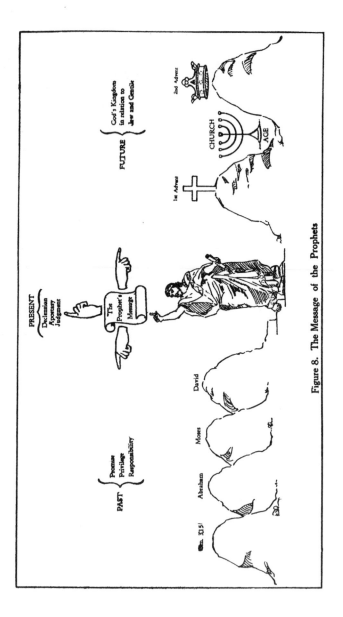

Figure 8. The Message of the Prophets

was to begin with Israel and Palestine and include the whole earth and its inhabitants. This redemption would be the fulfillment of the covenant made with Abraham.[4] They rebuked the people for their violation of the law of Moses, and when they broke the first two commandments accused them of spiritual adultery.[5] Looking back to David the prophets spoke of One coming from his house, who should be the universal king.[6]

The forward look. They were granted a two fold view of the Messiah, His sufferings,[7] and His exaltation.[8] From 1 Peter 1:10, 11

---

(4) Micah 7:20.—20 Thou wilt perform the truth to Jacob, and the mercy to Abraham, which thou hast sworn unto our fathers from the days of old.

(5) Jer. 3:20.—20 Surely as a wife treacherously departeth from her husband, so have ye dealt treacherously with me, O house of Israel, saith the Lord.

(6) Isa. 9:6,7.—6 For unto us a child is born, unto us a son is given: and the government shall be upon his shoulder: and his name shall be called Wonderful, Counsellor, The mighty God, The everlasting Father, The Prince of Peace. 7 Of the increase of his government and peace there shall be no end, upon the throne of David, and upon his kingdom, to order it, and to establish it with judgment and with justice from henceforth even for ever. The zeal of the Lord of hosts will perform this.

Ezek. 34:23,24.—23 And I will set up one shepherd over them, and he shall feed them, even my servant David; he shall feed them, and he shall be their shepherd. 24 And I the Lord will be their God, and my servant David a prince among them; I the Lord have spoken it.

Hosea 3:5.—5 Afterward shall the children of Israel return, and seek the Lord their God, and David their king; and shall fear the Lord and his goodness in the latter days.

Read Psa. 72 in connection with these references.

(7) Read Isa. 53.

(8) Jer. 23:5,6.—5 Behold, the days come, saith the Lord, that I will raise unto David a righteous Branch, and a King shall reign and prosper, and shall execute judgment and justice in the earth. 6 In his days Judah shall be saved,

we gather that the prophets were perplexed
when they attempted to reason out how the
Messiah could suffer and die, and yet be exalted.[9] Their perplexity was mirrored in the
experience of some old Jewish rabbis who felt
the difficulty of this problem, and as a solu-
tion taught that there were to be two Messiahs, Messiah ben Joseph, who should be
killed in a war with the Gentiles, and Messiah
ben David, who should come to reign in glory.
The prophets could not understand this peculiar revelation because to them was not
revealed the truth that there were to be two
comings of the Messiah, and that between
these advents there was to be a body of believers known as the Church, in which Jew
and Gentile should unite in the service of the
one God.[10]

WHAT THEY PREACHED

Notice the upper section of the chart.   The

and Israel shall dwell safely: and this is his name whereby
he shall be called, THE LORD OUR RIGHTEOUSNESS.

(9) I Peter 1:10, 11.—10 Of which salvation the prophets
have inquired and searched diligently, who prophesied of
the grace that should come unto you: 11 Searching what,
or what manner of time the Spirit of Christ which was
in them did signify, when it testified beforehand the sufferings of Christ, and the glory that should follow.

(10) Eph. 3:3-6.—3 How that by revelation he made known
unto me the mystery; (as I wrote afore in few words. 4
Whereby, when ye read, ye may understand my knowledge
in the mystery of Christ) 5 Which in other ages was not
made known unto the sons of men, as it is now revealed
unto his holy apostles and prophets by the Spirit; 6 That
the Gentiles should be fellowheirs, and of the same body,
and partakers of his promise in Christ by the gospel.

prophets had a message in relation to the past, present and future, as follows:

A *retrospective* message, dealing with the past. The prophets were the interpreters of Jewish history, using it as a background for their messages, and bringing home to the people the lessons contained therein.

A *forth-telling* message, dealing with the present. In relation to this aspect of their message, the prophets stand out as mighty preachers of spiritual religion. Sacrifices were divinely ordained, but when the people made the offering of these a substitute for works of righteousness, the prophets in Jehovah's name denounced the formality.[11] They re-

---

(11) Isa. 1:10-17.—10 Hear the word of the Lord, ye rulers of Sodom; give ear unto the law of our God, ye people of Gomorrah. 11 To what purpose is the multitude of your sacrifices unto me? saith the Lord: I am full of the burnt offerings of rams, and the fat of fed beasts; and I delight not in the blood of bullocks, or of lambs, or of he goats. 12 When ye come to appear before me, who hath required this at your hand, to tread my courts? 13 Bring no more vain oblation; incense is an abomination unto me; the new moons and sabbaths, the calling of assemblies, I cannot away with; it is iniquity, even the solemn meeting. 14 Your new moons and your appointed feasts my soul hateth: they are a trouble unto me; I am weary to bear them. 15 And when ye spread forth your hands, I will hide mine eyes from you; yea, when ye make many prayers, I will not hear: your hands are full of blood. 16 Wash you, make you clean; put away the evil of your doings from before mine eyes; cease to do evil; 17 Learn to do well; seek judgment, relieve the oppressed, judge the fatherless, plead for the widow.

Hosea 6:6.—6 For I desired mercy, and not sacrifice; and the knowledge of God more than burnt offerings.

Amos 5:21-24.—21 I hate, I despise your feast days, and I will not smell in your solemn assemblies. 22. Though ye offer me burnt offerings and your meat offerings, I will not accept them: neither will I regard the peace offerings

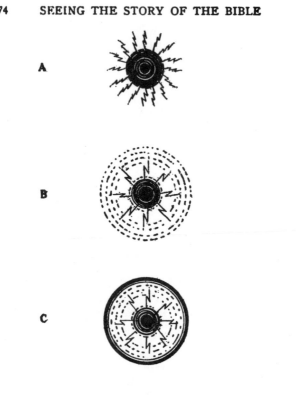

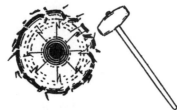

Figure 9. Spiritual Religion Imprisoned by Formalism
and Released by Prophets

buked that tendency in human nature which disposes it to substitute the sign for the thing signified, and to bow before the symbol rather than practise the thing symbolized. Many years ago it was reported that the Kentucky coffee tree which was growing in the Mississippi valley was threatened with extinction. The beans growing inside the pod had a shell so hard that the living germ in each had difficulty in getting out. So in Israel, there was a time when the hard shell of formalism was threatening to smother the germ of vital religion. Figure 9 on page 74 illustrates the degeneration of true religion into a dead ritualism and the prophet's ministry in relation to it. Diagram A symbolizes that living, radiant experience with which divine religion begins. In Figure B the dotted lines represent the forms and organization that are necessary to religion, but which have not yet stiffened so as to hinder. In Figure C we notice that form and organization have hardened into a solid cast that is slowly smothering the life of religion. Finally comes the prophet with the hammer of God's Word,[12] and delivers smashing blows upon this hard shell of ritualism.

---

of your fat beasts. 23 Take thou away from me the noise of thy songs; for I will not hear the melody of thy viols. 24 But let judgment run down as waters, and righteousness as a mighty stream.

(12) Jer. 23:29.—29 Is not my word like as a fire? saith the Lord; and like a hammer that breaketh the rock in pieces?

After the declension from a religion of practical righteousness, comes apostasy followed by the pronouncement of judgment.

A *fore-telling* message, dealing with the future. They spoke of the Day of the Lord, when Israel would be purified through tribulation and their enemies punished. Then would follow the kingdom of the Lord, when Israel would be gathered to Palestine under Messiah, and when the Gentiles would be converted and recognize Jerusalem as their spiritual center.

THE BOOKS THEY WROTE

We shall introduce to the reader these men of God whose ministry has been the theme of this chapter. We present to you:

Isaiah, the evangelist of the Old Testament, whose book abounds with predictions of the Messiah and His kingdom.

Jeremiah, the weeping prophet, whose ministry before the destruction of Jerusalem may be likened to that of a herald who goes before a condemned criminal, proclaiming his crime. He is the prophet who dipped his pen in tears to describe the destruction of the beloved city.

Ezekiel, the pastor of the exiles, who exercised a personal ministry to the Jews in Babylon when their national life was destroyed. He beheld the glory departing from the temple because of Judah's apostasy.

"Ichabod!" He saw it returning in the last days upon the millennial temple. *"Jehovah Shammah!"*

Daniel, the prophet of the Times of the Gentiles, who predicted the rise of the great empires of the world, and their fall at the coming of the kingdom of the Son of man.

Hosea, the heart-broken prophet, who, through his experience with an unfaithful wife, realized Jehovah's love for apostate Israel.

Joel, the prophet of Pentecost, who tells us that God will pour out His Spirit upon all flesh.

Amos, the shepherd prophet, who made a powerful plea for "old-time religion," where judgment would run like waters, and righteousness as a mighty stream.

Obadiah, the prophet of Edom's doom, who predicts the destruction of Judah's most implacable enemy.

Jonah, the missionary prophet, who learned through a strange and hard experience that God loves the Gentiles as well as He does Israel.

Micah, the people's friend, who rebuked the wicked indulgence of the ruling classes.

Nahum, the prophet of Nineveh's doom, who announced the destruction of Israel's most cruel oppressor—Assyria.

Habakkuk, the perplexed prophet, who failed to understand why Jehovah was so slow to punish His people for their wickedness, and was still more puzzled when told that the wicked Chaldeans were to be the instruments of judgment. He killed his doubts by standing upon the principle, "The just shall live by faith."

Zephaniah, the prophet of Josiah's revival, whose scathing denunciations helped to bring Judah to repentance.

Haggai and Zechariah, the Temple-building prophets, whose encouraging messages lifted the people from their indifference and fear, and moved them to complete the temple.

Malachi, the last of the Old Testament prophets, who utters the last exhortation of the Old Testament: to remember the law of Moses; and the last prediction, the coming of Elijah, Messiah's forerunner.

The "Tunnel" Period

In the concluding paragraph of Chapter IV mention was made of the "tunnel" of prophetic silence, lasting from the time of Malachi to the birth of Christ. Since this period of Jewish history is generally neglected by Christians, it will be profitable to present a summary of the history of the fortunes of the chosen people during those years.

A study of the Book of Esther will aid us in understanding God's relation to His people during this period. The strange feature of this book, describing the Jews' deliverance from a cruel enemy is that it does not contain the name of God. But although His name is not mentioned, His hand is clearly discerned. He is still with His people, though now hidden behind the scenes of history, controlling nations and individuals and secretly watching over His own. When Israel departed from Egypt, He delivered the nation with an open manifestation of His power; but in the story of this book, He remains concealed, working through natural channels and using human instruments. Such was His relation to the Jews during that period of four hundred years when there was no open vision given.

But the people did not enter this dark "tunnel" unilluminated. They were given two lights: a guide for the present, the law of Moses; and a hope for the future, the coming of Messiah preceded by Elijah His forerunner.[1] When the nation emerged, they found waiting for them a stern preacher of the law, John the Baptist, the one who ministered in the spirit and power of Elijah. He it was who presented to the nation, Jesus of Nazareth, the Messiah.

THE PERSIAN PERIOD (538 TO 333 B. C.).

After the period of the captivity, Babylon fell before Cyrus, king of Persia, whom God used to restore Israel to their land. Under Persian rule the Jews enjoyed peace. They returned from Babylon a cultured and literary people able to copy and disseminate the written Word. This task was committed in particular to a class of men known as the Scribes, of whom Ezra is the first mentioned in the Scriptures. Now that the fountain of living waters of inspiration had ceased, the work of the scribes became a kind of aqueduct to convey waters from the distant reser-

---

(1) Mal. 4:4-6.—4 Remember ye the law of Moses my servant, which I commanded unto him in Horeb for all Israel, with the statutes and judgments. 5 Behold, I will send you Elijah the prophet before the coming of the great and dreadful day of the Lord: 6 And he shall turn the heart of the fathers to the children, and the heart of the children to their fathers, lest I come and smite the earth with a curse.

voirs to the people. They later became expounders of the Scriptures, but their expositions were not especially inspiring, and were marred by a dependence upon tradition.[2] Still their work was to the Word what winter is to the seed, keeping it locked in the ground for the coming spring. Spiritually the period was characterized by formality in a worship led by a corrupt priesthood, and a growing national pride manifested in a contempt for the Gentile world.

THE GRECIAN PERIOD (332 TO 167 B. C.).

Alexander the Great, king of Macedonia, by his conquests became the founder of a mighty empire. Wherever he went he spread Greek culture and Greek language, thus paving the way for Christianity by providing a universal language. He treated the Jews kindly and

(2) Matt. 7:29.—29 For he taught them as one having authority, and not as the scribes.

Matt. 15:1-9.—1 Then came to Jesus scribes and Pharisees, which were of Jerusalem, saying, 2 Why do thy disciples transgress the tradition of the elders? for they wash not their hands when they eat bread. 3 But he answered and said unto them, Why do ye also transgress the commandment of God by your tradition? 4 For God commanded, saying, Honour thy father and mother: and, He that curseth father or mother, let him die the death. 5 But ye say, Whosoever shall say to his father or his mother, It is a gift, by whatsoever thou mightest be profited by me; 6 And honour not his father or his mother, he shall be free. Thus have ye made the commandment of God of none effect by your tradition. 7 Ye hypocrites, well did Esaias prophesy of you, saying, 8 This people draweth nigh unto me with their mouth, and honoureth me with their lips; but their heart is far from me. 9 But in vain they do worship me, teaching for doctrines the commandments of men.

encouraged them to settle in Alexandria, an Egyptian city founded by him. This city later became a great center of Jewish and Gentile culture, where scholars of both peoples taught and exchanged views. While in Egypt, the Jews began to translate their Scriptures into Greek, thus affording the Gentiles an opportunity of studying God's Word in a language spoken over a great part of the then-known world.

Greek ideas, customs, and speech began to be adopted by the Jews. They took Greek names, attended Greek games and studied Greek philosophy. Jehovah's people were menaced with a subtle danger. Greek culture, with its exalting of man and minimizing of sin was smothering Judaism. There was a general attitude of compromise and worldliness.

During this state of affairs there arose two classes among the Jews. The first, representing a "holiness movement" among the masses, were for a rigid separation from the Gentiles and their culture. Their aim was to protect the law of Moses from the heathen who would attack it and from the Jewish compromisers who would render it void. The second class, representing the worldy church party among the priesthood and nobles, were for comformity. Their aim was to remove from Jewish customs and religion whatever would be offensive to their heathen neighbors, and to dim the lines of separation. The first party dug a *ditch* to keep the Gentiles at a distance; the second built a *bridge* that invited fellowship. The first class was composed of devoted patriots with an ardent love for the law of Jehovah, the second, of easy-going worldlings, with no enthusiasm, little principle and no faith. The first party later were known as the *Pharisees*, the second as the *Sadducees*.

THE PERSECUTION UNDER ANTIOCHUS AND THE WAR OF INDEPENDENCE (166— 163 B. C.).

Deliverance came for the true religion in the form of a fierce persecution. The enmity of the Gentiles was to prove more healthful to Jews than their friendship. Antiochus Epiphanes, King of Syria, a peculiar combination of good and evil qualities, after suppressing a rebellion at Jerusalem, decided to destroy the Jewish religion. In so doing, he thought to break the national spirit and so prevent further disturbances. As if inspired by the Evil One, he defiled the Temple by offering a pig on its altar, ordered all copies of the Scriptures to be destroyed, and called upon the Jews to worship before heathen altars, with threats of horrible punishment for dissenters. Though many apostatized, thousands chose to suffer and die for their faith. The God of Israel had not taught His people in vain.

Finally, at the instigation of Mattathias, a

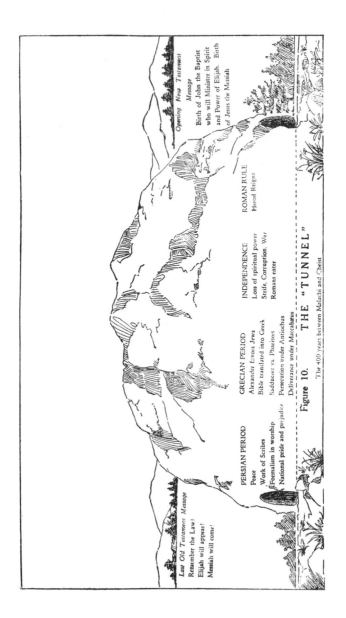

Law Old Testament Message
Remember the Law!
Elijah will appear!
Messiah will come!

PERSIAN PERIOD
Peace
Work of Scribes
Formalism in worship
National pride and prejudice

GRECIAN PERIOD
Alexander favors Jews
Bible translated into Greek
Sadducees vs. Pharisees
Persecution under Antiochus
Deliverance under Maccabeus

INDEPENDENCE
Loss of spiritual power
Strife, Corruption. War
Romans enter

ROMAN RULE
Herod Reigns

Opening New Testament
Message
Birth of John the Baptist
who will Minister in Spirit
and Power of Elijah. Birth
of Jesus the Messiah

Figure 10.   THE "TUNNEL"

The 400 years between Malachi and Christ

priest, the Jews rebelled. Under the leadership of his son, Judas Maccabaeus, the "Hammer," they defeated the Syrian armies and gained their independence.   Amid great rejoicing the Temple was cleansed and the ancient worship re-established.   The Jews have celebrated this deliverance in the Feast of Dedication ever since.

THE RULE OF THE MACCABEES. (162—40 B. C.).

For many years the country was ruled by priest-kings, the descendants of Mattathias. It soon appeared that in gaining their political freedom, the Jews had lost their spiritual power.   The reign of the Maccabees was marred by strife, civil war, Temple corruption, and persecution of the Pharisees.   Finally a quarrel among members of the reigning family led to an appeal to Rome.   This gave the Romans a wedge with which to force an entrance into the country, and in 63 B. C. they took possession of Palestine. They later placed on the throne a half Jew, half Edomite, Herod the Great, in whose reign was born the true King of the Jews, Jesus, the Christ.

VIII

Redemption Manifested

(The Four Gospels)

In the Old Testament we have seen Redemption prepared. In the New Testament we shall see:

Redemption manifested: the four Gospels.
Redemption truth propagated: the Acts.
Redemption truth explained: the Epistles.
Redemption's plan completed: the Revelation.

A WHOLE WORLD FOR THE WHOLE GOSPEL

The Redeemer, promised from the dawn of history, foreshadowed in the types of the Mosaic ritual, sung about in the Psalms and proclaimed by the Prophets, was sent forth "in the fullness of time," [1] at a time when the world needed Him and was in many ways prepared for Him. The same God who planted the gospel prepared the soil; He who had trained the Jews for their part in His redemptive program had also been working in history, preparing the Gentiles to receive the Good News. When Jesus appeared, the fol-

---

(1) Gal. 4:4.—4 But when the fulness of the time was come, God sent forth his Son, made of a woman, made under the law.

lowing conditions in the world of that day testified to its readiness:

There was a universal empire. The Romans by their conquests had welded the greater part of the known world into one great country where law and order were enforced and where towns were connected by good roads. Thus the preachers of the gospel could travel quickly from one country to another.

There was universal peace. The confusion and turmoil of war would have been a hindrance to the planting of the first seeds of Christianity.

There was a universal language. Greek was spoken throughout the Roman empire. The gospel, preached and written in this, one of the most perfect of languages, could be understood by people in all parts of the empire.

There was a universal need. "To corrupt and be corrupted is the spirit of the times," testified one Roman writer. People in general were longing for divine truth to light and guide them, for divine power to save them from their sins.

There was a universal expectation. The Jewish people, who were expecting the coming of the great King, carried this hope everywhere they went. In the East the expectation was general that a king should be born in Judea who was to rule the world.

A WHOLE GOSPEL FOR A WHOLE WORLD

The gospel was preached before the Gospels were written; Christian experience preceded the Christian Scriptures. For many years the world could hear the gospel from the lips of the apostles, that company especially appointed by the Lord to bear witness to the fact that the Jesus with whom they had walked on the roads of Galilee, was the same Jesus whom they had seen after His resurrection, and who was now dwelling in their hearts and lives by the Spirit.[2] Besides proclaiming this testimony, they taught the deeds and words of Jesus as the Spirit brought these to their remembrance.[3] Since their spoken witness would reach only their own generation, there arose a need for written records of the life and teachings of Christ so that the generations of the future should be able to have fellowship with those who had seen, heard and handled the Word of life.[4] To meet this need, the Lord inspired the writing

---

(2) John 15:27.—27 And ye also shall bear witness, because ye have been with me from the beginning.

Acts 1:21, 22.—21 Wherefore of these men which have companied with us all the time that the Lord Jesus went in and out among us, 22 Beginning from the baptism of John, unto that same day that he was taken up from us, must one be ordained to be a witness with us of his resurrection.

(3) John 14:26.—26 But the Comforter, which is the Holy Ghost, whom the Father will send in my name, he shall teach you all things, and bring all things to your remembrance, whatsoever I have said unto you.

(4) I John 1:1-3.—1 That which was from the beginning, which we have heard, which we have seen with our eyes, which we have looked upon, and our hands have

of four records of the life of the Master. Though Mark and Luke were not apostles themselves, yet there is evidence to show that they wrote their respective Gospels by apostolic authority.

Why *four* Gospels? A study of the Gospels and of the people of the age in which they were written would lead us to answer that *four* were written to meet in particular the needs of the four representative classes of that day (of course, *in general,* their message is for *all* ages and for *all* classes and nations). There was:

The Jew, the man of religion and prophecy, who was looking for a Redeemer promised in the Old Testament. To meet his need, Matthew wrote his book, to demonstrate that, Jesus of Nazareth, was He of whom Moses and the Prophets spake—the glory of Israel and light of the Gentiles.

The Roman, the man of government and conquest, whose ideal was a great general and conqueror. So in Mark's Gospel, Jesus is set forth as the mighty Conqueror, destroying the *real* enemies of mankind, sin and disease, and setting up by His death a spiritual empire in the hearts of men.

---

handled, of the Word of life; 2 (For the life was manifested, and we have seen it, and bear witness, and shew unto you that eternal life, which was with the Father, and was manifested unto us;) 3 That which we have seen and heard declare we unto you, that ye also may have fellowship with us: and truly our fellowship is with the Father, and with his Son Jesus Christ.

The Greek, the man of culture, whose aim was to develop man morally, mentally and physically, and whose ideal was the perfect man. Luke's Gospel meets this need by setting forth Jesus as the perfect divine Man, who became partaker of human nature in order that men might become partakers of the divine nature.

The Christian, the man of faith, who belonged to that new nation—the Church, composed of men of all nations. The first three Gospels may be described as *missionary Gospels,* assuming that they contained the substance of the messages preached from the beginning.[5] After churches had been established as a result of this preaching, there came a demand for deeper teaching concerning Jesus, on such topics as His Deity and the promise of the Spirit. To meet this demand, John wrote the *teaching Gospel,* in which Jesus is set forth as the eternal Son of God, the Word made flesh.

THE CHRIST OF THE GOSPELS FOR THE WHOLE WORLD

Let us imagine that as a missionary you have succeeded in reaching a tribe which has never before heard the story of Jesus. Because of the needs of other parts of the work

---

(5) Peter's sermon in Acts 10:36-43 contains a summary of Mark's Gospel: (1) The ministry of John the Baptist vv. 36, 37. (2) The ministry of Jesus v. 38. (3) His crucifixion v. 39. (4) His resurrection v. 40. (5) His appearance to the disciples v. 41. (6) The great Commission v. 42.

you can spend only a brief time with these people on this trip. You know, however, that you must tell the story in such a way that those who may die before you or some other missionary can return to them, will be able to believe unto salvation. How would you tell the story? We suggest the following:

Thirty Years of Waiting

The birth of Jesus' forerunner, John, was announced by an angel to Zacharias his father, who was performing his priestly duties in the temple. Then the same messenger came to Jesus' parents and told each at different times, that to them would be given a child, supernaturally begotten of God's Spirit, whose name was to be called Jesus, for He should save His people from their sins. This announcement came as a surprise to them, for at the time they were only engaged.

Humble shepherds were the first to have the joy of beholding the new born babe, who was to become the great Shepherd of men. Later, in the temple, two old Jewish saints, waiting for the coming of the Redeemer, gazed upon the child who was to be the glory of Israel and the light of the Gentiles. From the East came representatives of the Gentiles to worship the Babe, and to lay their gifts at His feet; typical of the time when the nations of the world were to bow before Him as King.

The enemy of mankind was not idle. His

attempt to destroy the virgin-born child, through the cruel king Herod, was foiled. The babe was taken for safety to a Gentile country, Egypt, and then to the humble Galilean town of Nazareth, where He grew to manhood. Just one story is told of His childhood days, in which we learn that at the age of twelve He knew that He was the Son of God, and that He was divinely called to a great work. For us, the next eighteen years are years of silence.

The Year of Small Beginnings

The great day came when Jesus was to receive His divine ordination to His mission, and to be publicly presented to the nation. He left Nazareth, and made His way to the place where His cousin John was preaching and baptizing people in preparation for the coming of the great King. As He, the sinless One, submitted to this rite, the Spirit's anointing for service came upon Him, and from heaven He heard the encouraging voice of His heavenly Father.

How should He use this power, and for what purpose? To settle these questions, He was divinely lead into the wilderness. There He resisted the enemy's sinful suggestions, and determined that His power should be used for the relief of suffering humanity, not for self; and that instead of worldly, political methods, He should employ spiritual; that instead of setting up His kingdom by the power of the sword, he should establish it by the loving power of His cross.

He then began His ministry and chose as His helpers humble fishermen. During this year He performed His first miracle, drove the money-changers and traders from His Father's house, and had an important interview with a great Jewish ruler, Nicodemus, who was seeking the way of salvation.

The Year of Popularity. The Crowds Gather.

The effect of Jesus' anointing received at the river Jordan was soon observed. As He manifested His power over disease, sin, death, demons, and nature, and as He taught and preached with an authority not seen in the religious teachers of that day, multitudes from all parts of the country began to gather to seek instruction and healing. Knowing that after His atoning death a great world-wide movement was to be established to spread His teachings and the good news of His salvation, He chose twelve men, known as apostles, whom He specially trained to become the first leaders of that movement. Besides these, He chose others to help Him in His work.

The Year of Opposition. The Crowds Leave.

The purity, truth, goodness, and self-sacrifice manifested in the ministry of the great Teacher encountered the opposition of human sin, pride, selfishness and ignorance. The Pharisees, the self-righteous religious party, opposed Him because He rebuked their formality and hypocrisy and because He mingled with the most sinful and degraded. The Sadducees, the political party, feared that His popularity might lead to a rebellion which would cause the Romans to take away the limited freedom that the nation enjoyed. The people, though acknowledging that He was a great prophet, did not accept Him as the promised King and Redeemer because He taught that His kingdom was a spiritual kingdom to be set up in the hearts of men, while they expected an earthly kingdom to be established with force of arms. Even His own relatives misunderstood Him. His popularity reached its height at the supernatural feeding of five thousand people, but He struck its death blow by refusing at that time to be made king at the request of the multitude, and by preaching that He had come to die that they might have life. Many of His followers left Him. After Peter's confession that He was the Messiah and Son of God He revealed to His followers His coming sufferings and death. To encourage them after this new and disheartening revelation, He permitted some of their number to see Him glorified, as a pledge of His coming glory. After the raising of a man from the dead had made Him popular for a time at Jerusalem, the rulers in council determined to put Him to death.

The Cross and the Crown

Though rejected, the King offered Himself to the nation on His triumphal entry into Jerusalem. Knowing that His time was at hand, He partook of His last supper with His disciples, delivered His farewell discourses, and went to the garden of Gethsemane, where in agony of prayer He testified to His willingness to do the Father's will. There He was arrested, and after a trial before the Jewish council and the Roman governor, was condemned to be crucified as a blasphemer and lawbreaker. He died on the cross, and was buried. But the grave could not hold Him who was the Prince of Life. On the third day He rose triumphantly, appeared to His disciples, and commanded them to preach the good news of His redeeming sacrifice to all the world after that they had received the power of the Spirit.

"What is the *meaning* of this story in relation to *me?*" we may imagine the people asking. Then, with confidence and gladness we can answer: "For God so loved the world, that He gave His only begotten Son, that whosoever believeth in Him should not perish, but have everlasting life."

The Outline of the Life of Jesus

THIRTY YEARS OF PREPARATION

Annunciations, Prophecies.

The Birth of Jesus.

The Babe worshiped by Jews and Gentiles.

The Babe, unnoticed by religious leaders; threatened by the king.

Flight to Egypt.   Childhood in Nazareth.

YEAR OF OBSCURITY: SMALL BEGINNINGS

Jesus' baptism. His temptation. First followers. First miracle. Cleansing of temple. Interview with Nicodemus.

YEAR OF POPULARITY: CROWDS GATHER

Jesus preaches, teaches, heals. Manifests His power over: Disease, Sin, Death, Demons, Nature.   Chooses the twelve apostles.

YEAR OF OPPOSITION: THE CROWDS LEAVE

Jesus opposed by Pharisees and Sadducees.

Misunderstood by people and by relatives.

Feeding of 5,000—height of popularity.

  Sermon on Bread of Life—death blow to popularity.

Peter's confession.   Coming death announced.

Transfiguration: pledge of coming glory.

Jewish council decides on Jesus' death.

THE CROSS AND THE CROWN

The triumphal entry—"Behold the King."

The Last Supper—"I go away."

Gethsemane—"Thy will be done."

Betrayal and arrest.

Trial and condemnation.

The crucifixion—"It is finished."

The resurrection—"He is risen!"

The ascension—"I ascend . . . tarry ye! . . . Go ye!"

How the Good News Was Spread
(The Acts of the Apostles)

The Book of Acts contains the history of
the establishment and growth of the church.
It describes how according to Christ's command and by the power of the Spirit the Good
News of salvation was preached to all nations.
Three keynotes are struck in the record, and
these sum up briefly the message of the book:

The Ascension of Christ: power for
world-evangelization made available.

The Descent of the Spirit: power for
world-evangelization imparted.

The Extension of the gospel: power for
world-evangelization made effective.

A careful study of the book will show
that its narratives gather round two individuals, Peter and Paul, the apostles, respectively, to the Jews and Gentiles. This would
suggest one purpose of the author, which was
to show how Jew and Gentile, long separated,
became one body in Christ.

Observe Figure 11 on page 99, in which is
illustrated the plan of the Book of Acts. The
circle at the top of the diagram contains the
key-verse, which presents the theme of the

book: "But ye shall receive power after that the Holy Ghost is come upon you: and ye shall be witnesses unto me both in Jerusalem, and in all Judea, and in Samaria, and unto the uttermost part of the earth." [1]   The dotted lines proceeding from the circle symbolize three representative outpourings of the Spirit, in relation to the three spheres of evangelization: Jewish, Samaritan, and Gentile.

In our study of the plan of the Book of Acts we shall first of all notice:

THE ESTABLISHMENT OF THE JEWISH CHURCH (CHS. 1-7)

This is represented on the chart by the figure of a Jewish synagogue.   The account is as follows:

Chapter one is really the introduction to the Acts.   The story itself begins with the arrival of the day of Pentecost. A sound as of a rushing mighty wind, the appearance of tongues of fire, the preaching of the gospel in languages miraculously given—and the Church was anointed for her world-wide ministry.   The first sermon delivered by the first preacher of the first church on the first day of her spiritual organization, brought in three thousand converts.

The primitive Christians were a happy and consecrated group.   So real was their unity

---

(1) Acts 1:8.—8 But ye shall receive power, after that the Holy Ghost is come upon you: and ye shall be witnesses unto me both in Jerusalem, and in all Judæa, and in Samaria, and unto the uttermost part of the earth.

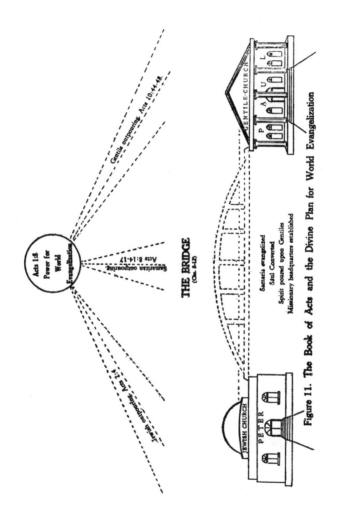

Figure 11. The Book of Acts and the Divine Plan for World Evangelization

at the beginning that they held all things in common—an ideal arrangement that was not to last. When a danger did threaten that unity, as in the case of the neglect of the Greek-speaking widows, the difficulty was soon settled in the spirit of love, sympathy and co-operation. Their fellowship, the reality of their experience, the working of miracles, drew many into the fold. Those who joined them in those days were generally sincere and genuine, for the death of Ananias and Sapphira had demonstrated to all that the church was a holy institution where hypocrisy would be quickly detected and punished. As was to be expected, the Jewish religious leaders attempted to prevent the spread of the Glad Tidings; but they were powerless to quench the gospel fire.

As yet, the church was a Jewish institution, the members of which had not grasped in all of their fullness the truths of the universality of the gospel and the passing of the old dispensation. Stephen, one of the Seven, had the largeness of vision and boldness to preach openly the abrogation of the Mosaic covenant. Unable to resist his wisdom the unbelieving Jews answered with the argument of violence. After the mockery of a trial, Stephen was condemned as a blasphemer. With the light of another world on his face and with a prayer for his persecutors on his lips, the first martyr of the church went to his reward. In charge of the executing party was Saul the

Pharisee, who as Paul the Apostle was to become Stephen's successor and carry his message to the Gentiles.

THE TRANSITION PERIOD (8-12)

The truth that Jews and Gentiles should form one body was at first a mystery; [2] it became a clear revelation; [3] raised an acute problem, [4] but finally was realized. [5] On the chart, the bridge drawn with dotted lines symbolizes the passing of the gospel from the

---

(2) Eph. 3:4-6.—4 Whereby, when ye read, ye may understand my knowledge in the mystery of Christ. 5 Which in other ages was not made known unto the sons of men, as it is now revealed unto his holy apostles and prophets by the Spirit; 6 That the Gentiles should be fellowheirs, and of the same body, and partakers of his promise in Christ by the gospel.

(3) Read the story of God's dealings with Peter and Cornelius in Acts 10.

(4) Read the story of Paul's controversy with the Jewish legalists (Acts 15).

(5) I Cor. 12:13.—13 For by one Spirit are we all baptized into one body, whether we be Jews or Gentiles, whether we be bond or free; and have been all made to drink into one Spirit.

Eph. 2:11-18.—11 Wherefore remember, that ye being in time past Gentiles in the flesh, who are called Uncircumcision by that which is called the Circumcision in the flesh made by hands; 12 That at that time ye were without Christ, being aliens from the commonwealth of Israel, and strangers from the covenants of promise, having no hope, and without God in the world: 13 But now in Christ Jesus ye who sometimes were far off are made nigh by the blood of Christ. 14 For he is our peace, who hath made both one, and hath broken down the middle wall of partition between us; 15 Having abolished in his flesh the enmity, even the law of commandments contained in ordinances; for to make in himself of twain one new man, so making peace; 16 And that he might reconcile both unto God in one body by the cross, having slain the enmity thereby: 17 And came and preached peace to you which were afar off, and to them that were nigh. 18 For through him we both have access by one Spirit unto the Father.

Jewish church to the Gentile world, there to form the Gentile division of the universal church. The paragraphs that follow will describe the divinely appointed stages in the widening of the Gospel circle to include men of every nation.

Stephen's influence had made itself felt. Philip, another of the Seven, left the narrow Jewish circle to preach the gospel to the despised Samaritans. He preached Christ, signs followed, a revival resulted, and there was great joy. The circle of evangelization was widening.

As the great champion of Judaism, Saul the Pharisee journeyed to Damascus with the object of persecuting the Christians there. He little realized that he was about to become a preacher of the faith he was attempting to destroy. He still remembered the scene at the stoning of Stephen. Doubts began to assail him, a mental struggle ensued, conscience began to speak—and Saul desperately kicked against the goads. The struggle was mercifully cut short. A flash of blinding light, a glorious vision, a voice from heaven—then *Saul the Pharisee* ceased, and *Paul the Apostle* arose! God had removed a dangerous persecutor and had secured a missionary for the Gentiles.

The divine plan for Gentile evangelization was still advancing. While *Cornelius the Gentile* was praying in Caesarea he was granted a vision and a promise of salvation.

While *Peter the Jew* was praying in Joppa, he, too, was granted a vision, the meaning of which he did not grasp at the time. Gentile and Jew met, and then Peter understood. As he preached to those gathered in Cornelius' house, the hearts of the listeners were purified by faith and they received the gift of the Spirit. Peter and his companions now knew that God had accepted the Gentiles and had placed them on an equality with the Jews.

One more step and the preparations for Gentile evangelization were complete. Some of those who had been driven from Jerusalem by Saul's persecution reached Antioch, where their witnessing resulted in the founding of a church which became "Missionary headquarters," and from which Paul the Apostle was sent as a missionary. All was now ready for the preaching of the gospel to "the uttermost parts."

THE ESTABLISHMENT OF THE GENTILE CHURCH (CHS. 13-28)

The Gentile church is symbolized on the chart by the diagram of a Greek temple. The narratives in chapters 13 to 28 gather around the person of Paul, the first typical missionary of Christianity. They describe his labors, his sufferings, and those missionary journeys that resulted in the organization of Gentile churches in Asia and Europe. We shall notice the part he played in the working out of God's great program for the world.

He himself knew and testified that he was a divinely appointed instrument for the promotion of world evangelization.[6] All his labors were to the end that the blessing of Abraham might come upon the Gentiles, that they might receive the promise of the Spirit through faith.[7]

In his preaching he relates the gospel to the one plan of redemption contained in the Scriptures. He connects the message he preached with the first promise of redemption,[8] with the promise to Abraham,[9] with

---

(6) Acts 9:15.—15 But the Lord said unto him, Go thy way: for he is a chosen vessel unto me, to bear my name before the Gentiles, and kings, and the children of Israel.

Rom. 11:13.—13 For I speak to you Gentiles, inasmuch as I am the apostle of the Gentiles, I magnify mine office.

Gal. 1:15, 16.—15 But when it pleased God, who separated me from my mother's womb, and called me by his grace, 16 To reveal his Son in me, that I might preach him among the heathen; immediately I conferred not with flesh and blood.

(7) Gal. 3:14.—14 That the blessing of Abraham might come on the Gentiles through Jesus Christ; that we might receive the promise of the Spirit through faith.

(8) Gal. 4:4.—4 But when the fulness of the time was come, God sent forth his Son, made of a woman, made under the law.

Gen. 3:15.—15 And I will put enmity between thee and the woman, and between thy seed and her seed; it shall bruise thy head, and thou shalt bruise his heel.

(9) Gal. 3:6-16.—6 Even as Abraham believed God, and it was accounted to him for righteousness. 7 Know ye therefore that they which are of faith, the same are the children of Abraham. 8 And the scripture, foreseeing that God would justify the heathen through faith, preached before the gospel unto Abraham, saying, In thee shall all nations be blessed. 9 So then they which be of faith are blessed with faithful Abraham. 10 For as many as are of the works of the law are under the curse: for it is written, Cursed is every one that continueth not in all things which

the law of Moses,[10] with the promise made to David,[11] and with the message of the Prophets.[12]

He was a man of world-wide vision, whose ambition was to extend Christianity beyond its original home. His aim was to "preach the gospel in the regions beyond," [13] and he laid it down as a guiding principle in his work never to build upon another man's foundation,[14] but to establish new churches.

---

are written in the book of the law to do them. 11 But that no man is justified by the law in the sight of God, it is evident: for, The just shall live by faith. 12 And the law is not of faith: but, The man that doeth them shall live in them. 13 Christ hath redeemed us from the curse of the law, being made a curse for us; for it is written, Cursed is every one that hangeth on a tree: 14 That the blessing of Abraham might come on the Gentiles through Jesus Christ; that we might receive the promise of the Spirit through faith. 15 Brethren, I speak after the manner of men; Though it be but a man's covenant, yet if it be confirmed, no man disannulleth, or addeth thereto. 16 Now to Abraham and his seed were the promises made. He saith not, And to seeds, as of many; but as of one. And to thy seed, which is Christ.

Compare Gen. 12:1-3.

(10) Acts 26:22.—22 Having therefore obtained help of God, I continue unto this day, witnessing both to small and great, saying none other things than those which the prophets and Moses did say come.

(11) Acts 13:22, 23.—22 And when he had removed him, he raised up unto them David to be their king; to whom also he gave testimony, and said, I have found David the son of Jesse, a man after mine own heart, which shall fulfill all my will. 23 Of this man's seed hath God according to his promise raised unto Israel a Saviour, Jesus.

(12) Acts 13:27.—27 For they that dwell at Jerusalem, and their rulers, because they knew him not, nor yet the voices of the prophets which are read every sabbath day, they have fulfilled them in condemning him.

(13) I Cor. 10:16.

(14) Rom. 15:20.—20 Yea, so have I strived to preach the

He was the means, in God's hand, of averting a danger to the program of world evangelization. This danger came from *Jewish national exclusiveness* which threatened to reduce Christianity to a Jewish sect, and *Jewish legalism* which would have smothered the infant Gentile church with the heavy garments of Jewish ceremonies. The fifteenth chapter of the Acts records the "Waterloo" of those Jewish Christian teachers who insisted that Gentiles keep the law of Moses in order to be saved. After much disputation on the question a council was called at Jerusalem and the matter thrashed out. Paul stood uncompromisingly for Gentile liberty,[15] recounting the wonderful works God had done among the Gentiles, apart from their observance of the Mosaic law.[16] In this position he was supported by Peter.[17] The result was a

gospel, not where Christ was named, lest I should build upon another man's foundation.

(15) Gal. 2:1-5.—1 Then fourteen years after I went up again to Jerusalem with Barnabas, and took Titus with me also. 2 And I went up by revelation, and communicated unto them that gospel which I preach among the Gentiles, but privately to them which were of reputation, lest by any means I should run, or had run, in vain. 3 But neither Titus, who was with me, being a Greek, was compelled to be circumcised: 4 And that because of false brethren unawares brought in, who came in privily to spy out our liberty which we have in Christ Jesus, that they might bring us into bondage: 5 To whom we gave place by subjection, no, not for an hour; that the truth of the gospel might continue with you.

(16) Acts 15:12.—12 Then all the multitude kept silence, and gave audience to Barnabas and Paul, declaring what miracles and wonders God had wrought among the Gentiles by them.

(17) Acts 15:7-11.—7 And when there had been much dis-

victory for Paul and the cause of Gentile
liberty.

---

puting, Peter rose up, and said unto them, Men and brethren, ye know how that a good while ago God made choice
among us, that the Gentiles by my mouth should hear the
word of the gospel, and believe. 8 And God, which knoweth the hearts, bare them witness, giving them the Holy
Ghost, even as he did unto us; 9 And put no difference
between us and them, purifying their hearts by faith. 10
Now therefore why tempt ye God, to put a yoke upon the
neck of the disciples, which neither our fathers nor we
were able to bear? 11 But we believe that through the
grace of the Lord Jesus Christ we shall be saved, even as
they.

PAUL'S LETTERS
Romans
1 and 2 Corinthians
Galatians
Ephesians
Philippians
Colossians
1 and 2 Thessalonians
1 and 2 Timothy
Titus
Philemon

Hebrews (?)

GENERAL LETTERS
James
1 Peter
2 Peter
1 John
2 John
3 John
Jude

Figure 12. The Epistles Interpret the Cross

Redemption Truth Explained

(The Epistles)

In the Gospels we are given the facts that constitute the foundation of the doctrines of redemption. In the Acts we have seen that the proclamation of those facts resulted in the establishment of churches. With the founding of these churches arose the need for an interpretation of the Good News. Those who had felt the power of the Cross wanted to know more concerning its meaning, and the application of its principles to the duties and relationships of everyday life. It had saved them from the wrath to come; now they must learn what standards of conduct it laid down for the life that now is. To meet these needs the Epistles (letters) were written.

The following is a general statement of the subjects dealt with in the Epistles:

The Gospels tell the *story* of the crucifixion; the Epistles *interpret* the story and the Christ who is its theme. They explain how sinful men are placed in right relations with God through Christ's atoning work; and how through faith and by the power of God they are delivered from the guilt and power of sin.

The Gospels describe the holy character of Jesus, and record His teachings which exhort us to follow in His steps. The Epistles explain how justified people may become in character like the Christ who saved them—how *saints* may become *saintly*. They assure the believer that by God's grace he can "put off concerning the former conversation the old man, which is corrupt according to the deceitful lusts," and that he can "put on the new man, which after God is created in righteousness and true holiness." They assure him that as he walks in the Spirit, there shall be manifested in his life the fruit of the Spirit, which is love, joy, peace, longsuffering, gentleness, goodness, faith, meekness and temperance.

The Epistles reflect the character of the teachings of Jesus in that they are intensely practical as well as deeply spiritual. They show the believer how to apply his faith and spirituality to the tasks, duties and problems of everyday life—how to practise his Christianity in church, state, family, social and business relations. While they exalt faith as the only means of access to God and the obtaining of the necessities of the spiritual life, they also insist that "faith without works is dead."

They set forth the nature and mission of the Church of Christ, and explain the dignity, duties and responsibilities of the Christian ministry. "But these things I write unto thee . . . that thou mayest know how thou oughtest to behave thyself in the house of God, which is the church of the living God, the pillar and ground of the truth." [1]

From the earliest days of Christianity the enemy of the Truth began to sow tares in the form of false teachers and erroneous doctrine. Danger to Christian doctrine came from the two sections composing the church: the Jewish and the Gentile. From the Jewish side the danger was *legalism,* an insistence that the keeping of the law was necessary to salvation and sanctification.[2] From the Gentile side there was the danger of *moral lawlessness,* a turning of the liberty of the gospel into license;[3] there was also the menace of *Gentile philosophy,* which would have caused Christianity to evaporate into a beautiful but powerless theory.[4] Therefore the Epistles "contend earnestly for the faith which was once delivered unto the saints."

They keep before the Christians the blessed Hope that will consummate their salvation— the coming of Christ. They explain this doctrine in relation to the church and the world, and emphasize its practical side, telling us that "the grace of God that bringeth sal-

(1) I Tim. 3:14, 15.
(2) Read the letter to the Galatians.
(3) Read the letter of Jude.
(4) Col. 2:8.—8 Beware lest any man spoil you through philosophy and vain deceit, after the tradition of men, after the rudiments of the world, and not after Christ.
Read I Cor. 2.

vation hath appeared unto all men, teaching us that denying ungodliness and worldly lusts, we should live soberly, righteously and godly in this world; looking for that blessed hope, and the glorious appearing of the great God and our Saviour Jesus Christ."[5]

---

(5) Titus 2:11-13.

The Plan Completed
(The Book of Revelation)

The great circle of the story of redemption begun in Genesis is completed in the last book of the Bible, Revelation. This will be seen from the following comparison:

GENESIS	REVELATION
Paradise lost.	Paradise regained.
Satan's entrance.	Satan's doom.
Beginning of the curse.	No more curse.
First tears.	All tears wiped away.
Beginning of conflict.	The final victory.
Divine communion broken.	Perfect fellowship.
Old heaven and earth.	New heaven and earth.

BACKGROUND AND MESSAGE

The books of the New Testament were written first of all to meet an immediate need of people living in the first age of Christianity, and also to convey a message to Christians of all time. A study of the conditions under which the different books were written will furnish a historical background that will make their messages clearer to us who live in modern times. For example, unless we know what was happening in the Galatian church in Paul's day, unless we know something of the methods and the activities of the Judaizers, we shall not grasp the full force of the message contained in the letter to that church. In order fully to appreciate and understand the message of Revelation let us see what crisis in the experience of the early church called forth this inspired prophecy. When this book was written the fires of persecution were fiercely burning.[1] The Roman empire with all its power was arrayed against God's little flock. Because Christians refused to worship idols they were accused of atheism; because they refused to worship before the image of the emperor they were branded as disloyal. Christianity was declared a menace to State, and a determined effort was made to destroy it. Out of the sufferings of those days came the questions, "Shall the kingdoms of this world destroy the kingdom of Christ? Shall the emperor of Rome triumph over Christ?" The heavenly answer was granted in the Book of Revelation which teaches that the kingdom of Christ shall ultimately triumph over all opposition, and that in the time of the end the kingdom of Antichrist (of which pagan Rome was but a type) shall be destroyed at the appearing of Christ. "Behold he cometh with clouds; and every eye shall see him and they also which pierced him: and all the kindreds of the earth shall wail because of him." [2]

(1) Rev. 1:9.—9 I John, who also am your brother, and companion in tribulation, and in the kingdom and patience of Jesus Christ, was in the isle that is called Patmos, for the word of God, and for the testimony of Jesus Christ.
(2) Rev. 1:7.—7 Behold, he cometh with clouds; and ev-

THE NATURE OF THE BOOK

It is a *book of power*. The saints are granted visions of the power of the unseen world, and are given the assurance that all power in heaven and earth shall be employed by God to establish His kingdom on earth.

It is a *throne book*. We are granted a vision of the throne of the great King, conveying the lesson that the heavens do rule. Thrones are promised to those overcoming the world with its subtle temptations.

It is a *crown book*. We see Christ crowned as King of kings, and the overcomers crowned and reigning with Him on earth.

It is a *book of conflict*. The great struggle foreshadowed in Genesis 3:15, experienced in all ages, reaches its final stage when Christ and Antichrist, representing respectively the power of God and the power of Satan, meet in conflict.

It is a *book of victory*. The Christ who once stood before earthly judges and rulers, now comes in power to execute righteous judgment upon all rulers.[3] The meek, once despised and downtrodden, now inherit the earth. The little flock receive the kingdom

---

ery eye shall see him, and they also which pierced him : and all kindreds of the earth shall wail because of him. Even so, Amen.

(3) Rev. 19:11-16.—11 And I saw heaven opened, and behold a white horse; and he that sat upon him was called Faithful and True, and in righteousness he doth judge and make war. 12 His eyes were as a flame of fire, and on his head were many crowns; and he had a name written, that no man knew, but he himself.

prepared for them from the foundation of the world. "The kingdoms of this world are become the kingdoms of the Lord, and of his Christ; and he shall reign for ever and ever." [4]

It is a *book of redemption.* The slain Lamb is the center of God's plan, and the object of the worship of all creation.[5] It is the slain Lamb who prevails to open the book that tells of earth's redemption. By His blood the saints are redeemed, in it they wash their robes, and by it they overcome the Accuser of the brethren.

THE STORY OF THE BOOK

Eliminating parenthetical passages, we shall attempt to trace the one main story that

---

13 And he was clothed with a vesture dipped in blood: and his name is called The Word of God. 14 And the armies which were in heaven followed him upon white horses, clothed in fine linen, white and clean. 15 And out of his mouth goeth a sharp sword, that with it he should smite the nations: and he shall rule them with a rod of iron: and he treadeth the winepress of the fierceness and wrath of Almighty God. 16 And he hath on his vesture and on his thigh a name written, King of kings, and Lord of lords.

Matt. 26:63, 64.—63 But Jesus held his peace. And the high priest answered and said unto him, I adjure thee by the living God, that thou tell us whether thou be the Christ, the Son of God. 64 Jesus saith unto him, Thou hast said: nevertheless 1 say unto you, Hereafter shall ye see the Son of man sitting on the right hand of power, and coming in the clouds of heaven.

(4) Rev. 11:15.—15 And the seventh angel sounded; and there were great voices in heaven, saying, The kingdoms of this world are become the kingdoms of our Lord, and of his Christ: and he shall reign for ever and ever.

(5) Read Rev. 5.

gives unity to this difficult book.   Consult Figure 13, on page 118.

THE UNVEILING OF THE CHRIST (CH. 1)

Just as at the dedication of a statue, the drapes are lifted that hide its true form from the public, so in the Revelation (which in Greek means "unveiling") Christ is unveiled before the eyes of His people, and shown as He is—the glorified One, the great Priest, King and Judge, and the Lord of the living and the dead.

CHRIST AND HIS CHURCH (CHS. 2, 3)

The great Overseer of the churches makes a tour of inspection to examine the lights of those whom He has appointed as "the light of the world."   He walks in their midst, commending, rebuking, comforting and making gracious promises.   He is especially active at this time, for the black clouds of tribulation are gathering, and the church must be ready for the crisis.   The time of the judgment of nations is approaching; but judgment must first begin at the house of God.

IN THE HEAVENLIES (CHS. 4, 5)

With John, our representative, we are caught up and given a place on the heavenly observation platform, from which point we shall view the scenes that are to take place on the earth before Jesus descends.   We see the throne of God, which teaches that He rules in sovereign power and will establish His kingdom on earth in spite of man's opposition.   We are given a view of the slain Lamb,

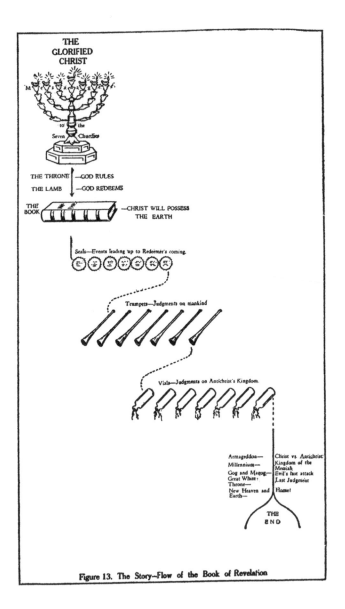

Figure 13. The Story—Flow of the Book of Revelation

symbolizing Him who, because of His atoning work, is worthy to open the book of earth's redemption.   He is the all-conquering Messiah, who can break the seals of the book, and put in motion those forces and bring to pass those events that shall lead to His triumphant advent, and the ushering in of the Messianic kingdom.

THE CRISIS OF THE AGES (CHS. 6-19)

Comparing Rev. 6 with Matt. 24:4-30 we may infer that seals describe the events which precede the coming of Christ.   Out of the seventh seal come the seven trumpets,[6] symbolizing severe hardening judgments to the nations.   Out of the seventh trumpet we may assume that the seven vials proceed. These represent the tribulation in the highest degree of intensity, and symbolize the judgments poured out upon the kingdom of Antichrist.

The seals, trumpets and vials describe in symbolic form that period known as the Great Tribulation.   We shall discuss this period from three different aspects:

We may compare the judgments of this period to a divine fire that will purify God's people who remain on earth, and that will destroy His enemies.

---

(6) Rev. 8:1, 2.—1 And when he had opened the seventh seal, there was silence in heaven about the space of half an hour. 2 And I saw the seven angels which stood before God; and to them were given seven trumpets.

We may describe this period as the time of "Satan's Pentecost." Antichrist, who is Satan in the flesh, is raised from the dead,[7] exalted,[8] and his coming and rule proclaimed to all nations by his executive, the false prophet.[9] The Satanic signs follow.[10] Satan then pours out of his spirit upon all flesh,[11] in

---

(7) Rev. 13:3.—3 And I saw one of his heads as it were wounded to death; and his deadly wound was healed; and all the world wondered after the beast.

(8) Rev. 13:4.—4 And they worshipped the dragon which gave power unto the beast: and they worshipped the beast, saying, Who is like unto the beast? who is able to make war with him?

(9) Rev. 13:11-17.—11 And I beheld another beast coming up out of the earth; and he had two horns like a lamb, and he spake as a dragon. 12 And he exerciseth all the power of the first beast before him, and causeth the earth and them which dwell therein to worship the first beast, whose deadly wound was healed. 13 And he doeth great wonders, so that he maketh fire come down from heaven on the earth in the sight of men. 14 And deceiveth them that dwell on the earth by the means of those miracles which he had power to do in the sight of the beast; saying to them that dwell on the earth, that they should make an image to the beast, which had the wound by a sword, and did live. 15 And he had power to give life unto the image of the beast, that the image of the beast should both speak, and cause that as many as would not worship the image of the beast should be killed. 16 And he causeth all, both small and great, rich and poor, free and bond, to receive a mark in their right hand, or in their foreheads: 17 And that no man might buy or sell, save he that had the mark, or the name of the beast, or the number of his name.

(10) Rev. 13:13.—13 And he doeth great wonders, so that he maketh fire come down from heaven on the earth in the sight of men.

(11) Rev. 16:13, 14, 16.—13 And I saw three unclean spirits like frogs come out of the mouth of the dragon, and out of the mouth of the beast, and out of the mouth of the false prophet. 14 For they are the spirits of devils, working miracles, which go forth unto the kings of the earth and of the whole world, to gather them to the battle of that great day of God Almighty. 16 And he gathered them

form of anti-Christian propaganda. This outpouring gathers his followers into an army that will oppose God and His hosts.[12]

Following the suggestion of S. D. Gordon, we may compare the happenings of this period to a great clearing storm. When two areas of sharply contrasted temperatures meet in the atmosphere, there is a storm. In like manner, when the power of Christ and the power of Satan clash in the last days, a terrific upheaval will take place in the spiritual and physical realms.

AFTER THE STORM (CH. 20)

There follows a period of calm and sunshine as the Sun of Righteousness rises over the horizon of the millennial day. God's kingdom comes on earth as predicted by the prophets. David's great Son reigns, executing perfect judgment. Man is undergoing his final probation in the midst of an ideal environment, where there is no want or oppression to disturb his peace and no Devil (for he is bound) to tempt him. But after a thousand years, Satan is loosed, and the powers of evil make

---

together into a placed called in the Hebrew tongue Armageddon.

(12) Rev. 13:4-6.—4 And they worshipped the dragon which gave power unto the beast: and they worshipped the beast, saying, Who is like unto the beast? who is able to make war with him? 5 And there was given unto him a mouth speaking great things and blasphemies; and power was given unto him to continue forty and two months. 6 And he opened his mouth in blasphemy against God, to blaspheme his name, and his tabernacle, and them that dwell in heaven.

their final onslaught, which is defeated. The great white throne is set up, and all are judged according to their works. Evil is swept from the earth and every man goes to his own place. We see a new heaven and a new earth.

HOME! (CHS. 21, 22)

The concluding scene of the Bible is one of home. After wandering for many millenniums, mankind (speaking in a general way) is at home in the great Father's house, enjoying perfect fellowship. There is manifested the mother-love of God for He wipes away all tears. We are given a view of the eternal home of the Lamb's wife, the New Jerusalem, which is to be the light of the world forever. The inhabitants of heaven and earth are gathered into one family, achieving that unity which consummates God's great plan.[13] God is now all and in all. As we leave the scene we may say with the old story writers, "And they lived happily ever afterwards."

---

(13) Eph. 1:9, 10.—9 Having made known unto us the mystery of his will, according to his good pleasure which he hath purposed in himself: 10 That in the dispensation of the fulness of times he might gather together in one all things in Christ, both which are in heaven, and which are on earth; even in him.

Eph. 3:14, 15.—14 For this cause I bow my knees unto the Father of our Lord Jesus Christ, 15 Of whom the whole family in heaven and earth is named.

I Cor. 15:24, 28.—24 Then cometh the end, when he shall have delivered up the kingdom to God, even the Father; when he shall have put down all rule and all authority and power. 28 And when all things shall be subdued unto him, then shall the Son also himself be subject unto him that put all things under him, that God may be all in all.

This completion of the divine purpose is still in the future; as yet we can only anticipate it.   But we can look forward to the time, when we shall review the plan in that place where we shall know even as we are known. Then we shall behold its perfection in a way at present impossible; in that day, with a hymn of praise to the wisdom of God, we shall be able to exclaim

"IT IS FINISHED!"

(SEE OVER)

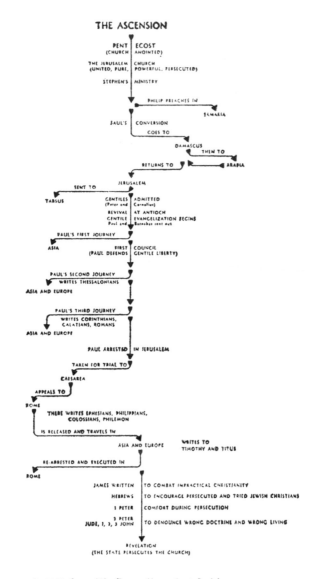

THE ASCENSION

PENT | ECOST
(CHURCH | ANOINTED)

THE JERUSALEM | CHURCH
(UNITED, PURE, | POWERFUL, PERSECUTED)

STEPHEN'S | MINISTRY

PHILIP PREACHES IN

SAMARIA

SAUL'S | CONVERSION

GOES TO

DAMASCUS
THEN TO

RETURNS TO | | ARABIA

JERUSALEM

SENT TO

TARSUS

GENTILES | ADMITTED
(Peter and | Cornelius)

REVIVAL | AT ANTIOCH
GENTILE | EVANGELIZATION BEGINS
Paul and | Barnabas sent out

PAUL'S FIRST JOURNEY

ASIA

FIRST | COUNCIL
(PAUL DEFENDS | GENTILE LIBERTY)

PAUL'S SECOND JOURNEY
WRITES THESSALONIANS

ASIA AND EUROPE

PAUL'S THIRD JOURNEY

WRITES CORINTHIANS,
GALATIANS, ROMANS

ASIA AND EUROPE

PAUL ARRESTED | IN JERUSALEM

TAKEN FOR TRIAL TO

CAESAREA

APPEALS TO

ROME

THERE WRITES EPHESIANS, PHILIPPIANS,
COLOSSIANS, PHILEMON

IS RELEASED AND TRAVELS IN

ASIA AND EUROPE | WRITES TO
TIMOTHY AND TITUS

RE-ARRESTED AND EXECUTED IN

ROME

JAMES WRITTEN | TO COMBAT IMPRACTICAL CHRISTIANITY

HEBREWS | TO ENCOURAGE PERSECUTED AND TRIED JEWISH CHRISTIANS

1 PETER | COMFORT DURING PERSECUTION

2 PETER
JUDE, 1, 2, 3 JOHN | TO DENOUNCE WRONG DOCTRINE AND WRONG LIVING

REVELATION
(THE STATE PERSECUTES THE CHURCH)

Fig. 14. The Stream of New Testament History — Acts to Revelation

STUDY QUESTIONS

As a help to the student and also to the teacher, we are adding a list of suggestive questions.

CHAPTER I

1. Describe and illustrate the method of study used in this book. (See Introduction.)
2. Does a superficial reading of the Bible give the impression of unity?
3. How many books are there in the Bible? Written by how many authors? Over what period of time? Name some of the subjects covered.
4. What do we discover after a repeated and careful reading of the Bible?
5. What feature makes the Bible different from the sacred books of other religions? For example, in what respect does it differ from the Koran?
6. Draw a chart illustrating the one theme connecting the many themes of the Bible.
7. Summarize briefly the story that constitutes the main theme of the Bible.
8. How does this story satisfy both mind and heart?
9. Did the inspired writers always see and understand God's full plan as each wrote his own particular section?
10. Did all the Bible characters understand that they were playing a part in God's drama of the ages?
11. Give an illustration showing how Christ is the center of the Scriptures.
12. Draw a diagram picturing the same truth.
13. How explain some of the differences between the Old and the New Testament?
14. What binds both Old and New Testaments together?
15. State briefly and clearly the relationship of the Old Testament to the New.
16. Draw a chart picturing this relationship.
17. Prove from Paul's preaching that the New Testament, before it was written, was contained in the Old Testament.
18. In what sense has the Old Testament passed away?
19. When was the fragrance of Old Testament truth made available for all the world?
20. Make a comparison of the two Testaments showing how the Old Testament is fulfilled by the New.
21. Explain how Christ causes the Old Testament to develop into the New.
22. Draw a diagram illustrating the above truth and be able to explain the diagram.

CHAPTER II

1. Give a brief outline of the book of Genesis, in three sections.

2. Draw the diagram of the book of Genesis and explain the development of God's plan step by step.

CHAPTER III

1. How does the book of Genesis conclude?
2. In what ways did Israel's experience of Egyptian bondage prepare them for their future mission?
3. Give an illustration explaining the reason and purpose of Jehovah's choice of Israel.
4. Why should Jehovah separate *one* nation as a chosen nation?
5. Describe the three sections of the law given at Sinai.
6. With what illustration do the prophets sometimes describe Jehovah's relationship to Israel?
7. What part did the law play in the plan of redemption?
8. How did Jehovah arrange for the Israelites to find Him always "at home"?
9. What was Israel's form of government? Then how may we describe the Tabernacle?
10. What was one purpose of the Tabernacle? What three important lessons did it teach concerning the character, will and purpose of Jehovah?
11. What elementary lessons did the Tabernacle teach the Israelites concerning the plan of salvation?
12. Why did the Tabernacle (or the Temple, which was its successor) finally pass away?
13. Draw a diagram illustrating the progress of the Divine plan of redemption.
14. In what Old Testament book do we read the rules of "Sacred Etiquette"?
15. Did Israel's failure in the wilderness spoil God's plan?
16. Draw a map illustrating Israel's journey from Egypt to the Promised Land.
17. Give the outline of this chapter.

CHAPTER IV

1. Into what two stages may the period from Joshua to Esther be divided? Describe the nature of each stage.
2. How did settlement in Canaan keep Israel separate?
3. What two other means did God employ to keep the people separate?
4. What good purpose did Israel's captivity and dispersion accomplish?
5. From what "disease" were the people clean on their return from Babylon?
6. What new truth did they learn about God?
7. What truth began to dawn upon them as a result of their contact with Gentile nations? Was it an entirely new truth?
8. Did they return to develop primarily a political life?
9. What resulted as they felt the pressure of Gentile powers?
10. How did they encourage themselves when the living prophets had ceased?

11. Describe the beginning of the institution later known as the Synagogue.
12. What drastic action did Ezra take to keep the people separated from the Gentiles?
13. Who took up the spiritual leadership of the people after the passing of the prophets?
14. Give an outline of this chapter.

CHAPTER V

1. Show the relationship between the three main sections of the Old Testament—History, Poetry, Prophecy.
2. Why is this chapter entitled, "The Heart of the Israelite"?
3. With what problem does the book of Job deal?
4. Why was the book written?
5. What kind of hymn-book did the Old Testament believers use?
6. What three kinds of "meetings" do we attend in the Psalms?
7. What was the purpose of the book of Proverbs?
8. What experience does the book of Ecclesiastes describe?
9. What is the message of the book?
10. What lesson is taught in the Song of Solomon?

CHAPTER VI

1. Did the prophets preach only concerning the future?
2. Contrast the office of prophet with that of priest.
3. Draw the diagram illustrating the message and vision of the prophet, and be able to explain it.
4. What led some of the rabbis to the conclusion that there must be two Messiahs?
5. Draw a diagram illustrating the release of vital religion by the ministry of the prophets. Explain the diagram.
6. Name the prophets and briefly summarize the message of each book.

CHAPTER VII

1. What Old Testament book illustrates God's attitude toward the Jews during the "tunnel" period?
2. What illumination was given the Jews as they passed through the "tunnel"?
3. Whom did God use to restore Israel to their land?
4. How were they treated by the Persians?
5. Describe the work of the scribes.
6. Give the date of the Persian period.
7. Give the date of the Grecian period.
8. Who was the founder of the Grecian empire?
9. How did he treat the Jews?
10. What great translation was made during this period?
11. What danger menaced the Jews during this period?
12. Who arose to combat this menace?
13. To what other party were they opposed?

14. Describe the persecution by Antiochus Epiphanes.
15. Did this persecution prove to be a blessing or a curse?
16. Describe the war of independence. Who was the leader of the Jews?
17. In what feast do the Jews celebrate their deliverance?
18. Give the date of the persecution and the war of deliverance.
19. Give the date of the rule of the Maccabees.
20. Describe their rule.
21. What led to the entrance of Rome?

CHAPTER VIII

1. Show the relation of the five sections of the Bible to the story of Redemption. See top of page 86.
2. In what five ways was the world prepared for His coming?
3. Since there was no New Testament in the early days of Christianity, who guaranteed the truth of the facts concerning Jesus?
4. Were Mark and Luke apostles?
5. Why *four* Gospels?
6. To whom was Matthew written? What message does the book convey? Give the same facts concerning the other three Gospels.
7. How may the first three Gospels be described? Why?
8. How may the Gospel according to John be described?
9. Give from memory, the *outline* of the Life of Christ.

CHAPTER IX

1. What does the book of Acts describe?
2. Give the three keynotes of the book.
3. Round what two great men do its narratives center?
4. Quote the key-verse.
5. Draw a diagram illustrating the plan of the book of Acts.
6. Tell the story of the establishment of the church.
7. Tell the story of the Transition Period.
8. Describe the work of Paul the apostle.

CHAPTER X

1. Draw a chart illustrating the connection between the Epistles and the Gospel story.
2. Describe the relationship between the Epistles and the Gospels.

CHAPTER XI

1. Show how Revelation completes the circle of Divine truth begun in Genesis.
2. What was happening to the church at the time of the writing of the Revelation?
3. What is the message of the book?
4. Describe the nature of the book.
5. Draw a diagram illustrating the line of thought in the book.
6. **Trace briefly the main line of thought in the book.**